*Just Talk
to Me*

BOOKS BY ANDRÉ BUSTANOBY—
*But I Didn't Want a Divorce*
*Just Talk to Me*
*The Readymade Family*

# Just Talk to Me

*The Principles and Practice*
*of Communication in Marriage*

André Bustanoby
with
Fay Bustanoby

**ZONDERVAN**
**PUBLISHING HOUSE**

OF THE ZONDERVAN CORPORATION
GRAND RAPIDS, MICHIGAN 49506

JUST TALK TO ME
© 1981 by The Zondervan Corporation
Grand Rapids, Michigan

Zondervan Publishing House, 1415 Lake Drive, S.E.,
Grand Rapids, Michigan 49506

**Library of Congress Cataloging in Publication Data**
Bustanoby, André.
    Just talk to me.
    Includes bibliographical references and indexes.
    1. Communication in marriage. I. Bustanoby, Fay, joint author. II. Rock, Louise H.
III. Title.
HQ734.B934        306.8'7        80-28835
ISBN 0-310-22181-1

*Edited and designed by Louise H. Rock*

*Printed in the United States of America*

84   85   86   87   88 — 10   9   8   7   6   5

# Contents

# Preface

Communication, like any other skill, can be learned. But it requires setting aside our fears, our prejudices, and our own way of doing things. This book is both a personal story and a "how to" book on communication.

In almost thirty years of marriage we have learned a lot about communication that we want to pass on to others. Some of these lessons we have learned by trial and error. Others we have learned from a study of the subject.

At the core of good communication is a respect for each other's differentness. My position is not *better than* yours; it is just *different from* yours. Once that concept is mastered, the techniques of good communication are easily mastered.

Good communication does not, however, require that you give up your beliefs and convictions. It does require that you hear the beliefs and convictions of others and be willing to listen with an attitude of respect and understanding.

André and Fay Bustanoby
Bowie, Maryland

# But I'm Supposed
# To Be Submissive

—By André

I HAD JUST FINISHED my lecture on communication in marriage and asked for questions when one woman raised her hand and said, "I appreciate what you've been teaching us about improving communication in marriage. But would you elaborate a bit more on the idea that a wife can be submissive and still speak up? I've been taught that submission means silence. If you don't like what you're husband's doing, you just grin and bear it, and the Lord will give you the strength."

This woman seemed to be speaking for many there. She and the others were confused over what seemed to be a contradiction between exhortations to speak up and the biblical teaching of the submissive role of the wife. What is more, from what they told me, many of their husbands conspired to keep them from speaking up by reminding them of the husband's headship.

*Hank and Betty's Problem.* Hank and Betty are typical of this kind of relationship. They both were new Christians and had been schooled in a very repressive view of the headship of the husband and the submission of the wife.

The only thing atypical about their story is the violence. Few Christian wives I have counseled have been abused physically, though I find that many of them are intimidated.

I experienced Hank as an intense man. He had played professional baseball for several years before he went into business for himself. He still keeps in shape by jogging and weight lifting. He cuts a fearsome figure as a man, and just talking with him was an intimidating experience. His eyes are penetrating, and he speaks with authority.

When he and Betty came for counseling, he did most of the talking. According to him, Betty had "an authority problem." By that he meant that she would not knuckle under and do what he wanted her to do. She was not being "a submissive Christian wife." He made it clear that I had a responsibility as a Christian counselor to convince her of her error.

Betty remained dutifully silent while Hank carried on the conversation and gave us a Bible lesson in how the Christian home ought to function. I had a hunch that if I let Hank go on long enough Betty would speak up. She managed to remain silent for about a half an hour, but I could tell that she was having a problem with something. Finally she said, "May I say something?"

She began quietly: "Hank isn't telling the whole story. The reason we're here is that I told him we either get marriage counseling or I leave. I just got out of the hospital for surgery on my knee. Two weeks ago Hank was furious with me for not being 'submissive' and shoved me down. My leg twisted, and I tore some ligaments "

Betty continued: "This wasn't the first time. I've been manhandled before. He shoves me around a lot and has me scared to death most of the time. He's promised not to touch me again, but I'm still afraid of him."

Hank spoke up: "I know I was wrong to shove her. I won't do it again. But she must do something about her problem with my authority. She finds it difficult to submit to me."

In the conversation that followed I realized that I wouldn't get very far in teaching new communication skills or problem solving until we got a new perspective on the "authority problem." I needed to correct their view of Ephesians 5:22–33 and First Peter 3:1–7. They were open to what I had to say, and further counseling revealed that they were applying what they had learned about the headship of the husband and the submission of the wife.

## THE HEADSHIP OF THE HUSBAND

According to Ephesians 5:22–33 the headship of the husband involves several specific duties. He is to be his wife's savior, sanctifier, nourisher, and cherisher.

*The Wife's Savior.* Ephesians 5:22–33 makes it clear that the wife is to be subject to her husband as the church is to be subject to Christ. And, the husband is to love his wife as Christ loved the church and gave Himself up for her. I understand the parallelism here quite literally. Christ is Head and Savior; the husband is to be head and savior.

To love your wife as Christ loves means to give yourself. That's what a savior does. A husband may not be required to lay down his life for his wife, but dying a little bit for her every day in terms of selfless giving certainly is in order.

Christ's example of washing the disciples' feet (John 13:1–20) deserves attention at this point. It stands not only as an example of the attitude believers are to have for each other but also the attitude husbands are to have toward their wives. I have often toyed with the idea of using footwashing in marriage therapy—particularly where the problem is a dominant, intense husband who demands that his wife knuckle under his authority.

Husband, think for a moment how patient, longsuffering, and kind Jesus Christ has been to you. Does that attitude typify your attitude toward your wife?

*The Wife's Sanctifier.* Paul teaches that the husband is not only the wife's savior but also her sanctifier (Eph. 5:25–27). The word "sanctify" has to do with holiness. When Christ died for us His intention was not only to deliver us from the consequences of our sins but also to make us a spotless bride fit for eternal companionship with Him.

The sanctification referred to here is not the church's or wife's *experience* of holiness—how she behaves. It is a *position* of holiness. When believers become the bride of Christ we at that moment are declared spotless and fit for Him who is sinless. We may not be spotless in *experience* or *behavior*. But as the bride of Christ, we have a *position of acceptance* as a spotless bride.

Now follow this carefully. In that position of acceptance, believers are given a climate in which they can grow in the experience of holiness. We are *unconditionally* accepted by faith in Christ. We have no conditions hanging over our heads that make us feel, "If I'm good enough He will accept me." No! The feeling is this: "Having been accepted by Him as His bride, *I want to* please Him."

What a profound correlation we have here for the human institution of marriage! This is exactly what Fay and I want to convey in the first part of this book—the importance of acceptance. It is in a context of acceptance that husbands and wives grow. We do not behave in order to be accepted. We behave because we are unconditionally accepted. We are secure in our relationship with God—and should be with each other.

*The Wife's Nourisher.* In Ephesians 5:22–27 the spiritual dimension of the husband/wife relationship is emphasized. The human side is emphasized in verses 28 and 29. The husband is instructed to love his wife as his own body. He is told to "nourish" her.

The word "nourish" means quite literally "to feed with nutriment for the purpose of growth." It has the wife's total welfare as a human being in view. It includes her physical, emotional, and intellectual growth. The husband is required to provide a climate where this human being called his wife can grow.

There's nothing repressive about this kind of headship! Here, the wife flourishes under his headship. She is ever growing as a human being. If submission results in the physical, emotional, and mental deterioration of the wife, then it is not *biblical* submission.

Husband, are you an impediment to, or a facilitator of, your wife's growth as a human being? Does your body crave rest and recreation? Then desire it for her also. Do you like to have your mind stimulated by new projects, by friends and travel? Then desire it for her. Do you like to go out to eat after a hard day of work and relax in a convivial atmosphere? Then desire it for her. The Christian husband loves his wife as his own body. He is a nourisher.

*The Wife's Cherisher.* The word translated "cherish" (Eph. 5:29) is used in classical Greek to describe a nurse holding a baby close, warming it with her body heat and rocking it. It is non-sexual body contact that gives physical and psychological warmth. Our vernacular would call it "cuddling."

The young woman in the Song of Solomon put it beautifully when she said:

Like an apple tree among the trees of the forest,
So is my beloved among young men.
In his shade I took great delight and sat down,
And his fruit was sweet to my taste (Song of Sol. 2:3).

How many husbands sit still long enough to provide shade and sweet fruit? If there is one complaint I hear more than any other from wives it is this: The husband doesn't know how to cuddle. When he is close to his wife he tends to think in sexual terms, which infuriates her when she wants only to be cuddled.

This is important not only to young couples but older couples as well. Family consultant Evelyn Duvall makes a powerful plea for this when she says,

> Less tangible but quite as important is the emotional building up that each gives the other through their everyday life together. Too frequent is the embittered couple bent on belittling and tearing each other down in the myriad assaults upon ego and self that only the intimate can inflict. More successful is the support of one another by husbands and wives who have built up patterns of mutual encouragement and appreciation upon which they both can lean as other faculties fail. . . . The husband who can make his wife feel his devotion and appreciation for all she has done and all she is helps her feel desired and desirable, more important than ever now in the sunset years. One explicit example of this is given in a report of a man who, on his fifty-fifth wedding anniversary, inserted the following advertisement in his local paper:
>
> To my sweetheart, Sophie Hensel, I wish to thank you publically for your love and devotion and for fifty-five years of wedded happiness made possible by your unmatched qualities as wife, mother, mother-in-law, grandmother, and great-grandmother. We all revere you.
>
> Your husband, Henry Hensel.[1]

It is no surprise to me that this marriage was so durable. Henry Hensel's style of leadership in the marriage comes through loud and clear.

## THE SUBMISSION OF THE WIFE

The biblical teaching of the wife's submission should be understood in an *organizational* rather than a personal sense. I mean this. Even though the Bible speaks of her submission to her husband in the *organization* of the marriage, *personally* she is as much the object of God's grace as her husband (Gal. 3:28; 1 Peter 3:7).

Christian marriage has two dimensions: the organizational dimension and the in-grace dimension. I call the first one "vertical" and the second "horizontal." The in-grace dimension is horizontal in that the husband and wife are equals in grace. The organizational dimension is vertical because the husband is to assume a special position of leadership under which the wife is to place herself. But we must be careful how we describe that leadership, otherwise in her submissive role the wife will be made to look like a second-class citizen.

Remember that the husband, following the example of Christ, provides for the wife a *position* in which she may grow and thrive as a Christian and as a human being. His failure to provide this opens up an entirely different set of problems, which I deal with in my book *But I Didn't Want A Divorce* (Zondervan).

All I'm attempting to establish here is the context in which submission is taught. The wife's place of growth is in the climate the husband establishes for her, functioning as her savior, sanctifier, nourisher, and cherisher. I have yet to find a Christian wife who is unwilling to let her husband provide that kind of climate, or who is not content to grow in it. The complaints I hear are just the opposite. The husband *fails* to provide such a climate for her.

Now growth in that climate is to be accompanied by specific behavior in the wife. And this behavior is especially important when the husband doesn't do a very good job of providing a climate for her growth.

First Peter 3:1–7 offers some guidance for her. Peter's advice is given in the case of the believing husband who doesn't act in his wife's best interest (1 Peter 3:1). Three things are important to this central passage: 1) the husband's failure and the wife's behavior, 2) illustrations of chaste and respectful behavior, and, 3) the husband's two-fold responsibility to his wife.

*The Husband's Failure and the Wife's Behavior.* When the husband fails to provide a climate for his wife's well-being and growth, the wife is not to nag him. She is rather to make impact with her behavior, which is described as "chaste and respectful" (1 Peter 3:2).

Let me make it very clear that I do not think that the submissive wife is to be a *silent* wife. A healthy marriage requires that she speak up. The *attitude* is all important. This will govern *how* she communicates.

I understand "chaste" behavior as being more than personal holiness. It is a quality of life that actually awakens in the husband religious awe. Is your husband awe-struck by you—or is he struck by other things?

The "respectful behavior" is simply deference to his *position* as head of the household. According to First Peter 3:7 he is to realize that his wife is a "weaker vessel," and because of this he is responsible to God for his behavior. Peter is saying that there are burdens and responsibilities in the marriage that the husband, not the wife, must bear. He is to be the strong one, the leader, and the protector. But suppose he doesn't take this responsibility seriously? Suppose he puts the burden of leadership on his wife? Suppose she is left with the responsibility of keeping the family, the house, and the car going while he retreats to a private life of his own? Suppose when she tries to get him to carry some of the load he simply does nothing or says, "Do whatever you want, dear"? Is his wife going to take up the slack or nag him for not assuming his responsibilities in the marriage? No, she must say, "He is supposed to be giving leadership to the marriage and family. He is responsible for keeping the family, the car, and the house going. I will help, but I will not take the leadership. If the bills don't get paid, if the car doesn't get serviced, and if the rain floods the basement and ruins the furnace, then he'll have to face the consequences." This is what I mean by deference to his position as the head of the household. The wife is not to nag the husband or take the responsibility on herself. She must let him take the consequences of his irresponsibility.

Often the Christian wife makes the same mistake the wife of the alcoholic makes. She facilitates her husband's delinquency by bailing him out. He can be delinquent because his wife will cover for him.

The delinquent husband, whether alcoholic or not, must not be mothered. The wife in a position like this must practice "loving disengagement." Her attitude must be, "I care what happens, but I won't facilitate his irresponsibility by doing what he should do." I'm aware that some husbands pull mothering from their wives. For example, when he fails to have the car serviced or the flooded basement repaired and goes off to play golf like an irresponsible little boy, the wife becomes a "mother" and does what her irresponsible "little boy" has failed to do. But when she falls into that trap and mothers him, he does just as the alcoholic does and turns on his wife. He blames her for his failure to act because she takes away the initiative from him.

Now the wife knows that's not true. But she gives him ground to accuse her because she assumes his responsibility. She must not do that.

Irresponsibility is to be handled with this kind of man exactly as it is done with the alcoholic. The wife is not to nag him or do what he is responsible for doing. She must permit his irresponsibility to take its inevitable course and let his world fall down around him.

The wife may object and say, "But we're married, and my world falls down *too.*" It is true that things will get worse for her before they get better. But a problem like this requires strong medicine with some painful side-effects.

*Illustrations of Chaste and Respectful Behavior.* Peter uses two illustrations of chaste and respectful behavior.

The first is that of jewelry. Peter suggests that the wife wear the adornment of a gentle and quiet spirit. This has to do with attitude. It is the kind of attitude I described as "loving disengagement." This does not mean that the wife is to sit by passively while her husband destroys her. All earthly authority has its limits, whether it's civil and ecclesiastical authority

(Acts 5:17–32) or the authority of the husband (1 Cor. 7: 10–11).[2]

Peter gives a second illustration—that of Sarah (1 Peter 3:5–6). On two occasions Abraham, a believing husband, seriously failed Sarah. On both occasions, to save his own skin, he denied she was his wife. In both cases God intervened (Gen. 12:10–20; 20:1–18).

Peter is encouraging the wife in submission not to be too quick to act on her own behalf when the husband fails. She may argue that if her husband doesn't pay the bills their credit will be ruined. But maybe her husband needs to have creditors hounding him instead of his wife hounding him. Or she may say, "The engine in the car will be ruined if it's not given service." Maybe her husband needs to experience the inconvenience and expense of a ruined engine. God can use other people and circumstances to get to a husband like this if the wife will let Him. I think that it would be going a bit far to say that God *never* wants a woman to act in her own interest when her husband jeopardizes her welfare. First Corinthians 7: 10–11 indicates otherwise. He is simply saying, "Don't be too quick to act on your own behalf. If God wants to intervene directly, give Him a chance to do so." The warning to husbands that they had better act in their wives' interests also seems to bear this out (1 Peter 3:7).

*The Husband's Two-Fold Responsibility to His Wife.* The teachings of First Peter 3:1–6 are to be understood in the light of verse 7. Effective communication and a workable marriage cannot be achieved by the wife's effort alone.

In First Peter 3:7 the husband is given two distinct responsibilities that reinforce what Paul says in Ephesians 5. The husband is: 1) to live with his wife, understanding that she is "a weaker vessel," and, 2) to assign her a place of honor as a fellow-heir of the grace of life.

Whatever Peter means by "weaker vessel," he certainly doesn't mean that she is inferior. I think that this should be understood as having liabilities as a human being that the husband does not have. Here are some of them.

a) Physical liabilities—Women have fifty percent less brute strength than men. They have smaller lungs, twenty percent fewer red blood cells and a lower vital capacity or breathing power in the 7:10 ratio. Their constitutional viability is therefore a long-range matter. When the working day in British factories, under wartime conditions, was increased from ten to twelve hours, accidents of women increased 150 percent, but of men not at all.[3]

b) Physiological—In functions, women have several very important ones totally lacking in men—menstruation, pregnancy, and lactation. All of these influence behavior and feelings. She has more different hormones than man. The same gland behaves differently in the two sexes—thus woman's thyroid is larger and more active. These distinctive functions contribute to wide emotional swings—she laughs and cries more easily than man.[4]

c) Psychological—Males are more aggressive. The sex difference in aggression has been observed in all cultures in which the relevant behavior has been observed. Boys are more aggressive both physically and verbally. This difference is not to be traced to the socialization of the male—that boys are supposed to be that way. It is rather a biological function. Male hormones (androgens) function during prenatal development to masculinize the growing individual. Genetic females exposed to abnormally high (for females) levels of androgens prenatally are masculinized both physically and behaviorally, including elevated levels of threat behavior and rough and tumble play.[5]

The combination of brute strength and native aggressiveness certainly places the male in a position to enforce his will. But Christian marriage is designed to mitigate this.

When Peter speaks of the wife as a "fellow-heir of the grace of life" he means this. All the good things God gives us—material, spiritual, and physical—the wife has as much right to as the husband. She is to share equally.

Patricia Gundry in *Heirs Together* puts a necessary emphasis on this when she says;

> He was to *grant* her this honor; otherwise she did not have it. And how could she be a fellow-heir? He had to lift her up and treat her as an equal, a co-heir with him in life. He would be treating her in an uncommon way, but he would be living out his faith, a faith which leveled all social barriers, even those between husbands and wives.[6]

*Summary.* Effective communication can be learned and practiced only in a climate of acceptance. The biblical teaching of the headship of the husband and the submission of the wife creates such a climate.

As a leader-servant the husband establishes such a climate in the organization of the marriage. And, recognizing his wife as a fellow-heir of the grace of life, he respects her as an individual who is as much the object of God's grace as he.

The wife, understanding the responsibility of the husband in the organization of the marriage, treats him with deference. Her attitude is such as to provide an opportunity for his leadership. She is not quick to act apart from him. I have pointed out, however, that she may have to act on her own behalf when the marriage has deteriorated beyond repair.

## 2

# "Back to Square One After Twenty-seven Years"

### —By André

On February 19, 1979, it was still snowing. For three days the snow, driven by gale winds, had gradually paralyzed the Washington, D.C., metropolitan area. All transportation was stalled; all appointments cancelled. But I had no excuse not to go to work. My office is in my home.

It was Monday, and I sat in my study staring out of the window, feeling a bad case of the February blues coming on. "It's not snowing in southern California," I thought.

My mind went back to the happy times Fay, our boys, and I spent surfing and swimming on California's beautiful beaches. Fay and I had often talked about going back to southern California and opening a home for troubled boys. We've always had a special place in our hearts for boys, having four sons of our own. And we enjoyed their friends too, both in our own home and at the sports events at high school. One friend stayed over at our house so much he practically lived there.

We were also into the Orange County foster parent program and took in two girls. At one time we had our four boys and three foster children living with us—five teens in the house at one time. We loved it.

Now as I watched the snow from my study window I wanted to renew those happy times. "Why not?" I thought. So I picked up the phone and called San Diego information. "Please let me have the number of the San Diego County Department of Welfare."

After several calls I finally contacted the agency that licensed group homes. Yes, it would be possible to get a license to run a group home if it were set up as I proposed.

Another call to Orange County right outside of Los Angeles received the same response. A group home would be a possibility in either Orange County or San Diego County.

I got out a map. Even on paper, southern California looked good, with all those familiar, warm-sounding names: Palm Springs, San Diego, Oceanside, Newport Beach!

My mind turned back to the notes on my desk: "Sharpen pencil and make cost estimates and budget projections."

As my excitement grew, my February blues faded. Only for a moment did I hesitate.

"Lord, my motive isn't so great is it? Escape from the snow, huh?"

Then, after pondering this a bit, I said "No, Lord. That's not all it is. You know that You, Fay, and I have talked about this a lot. My motive isn't just to get out of this snow." My hesitation passed, and I turned to my figures.

*A Painful Encounter.* Fay was sitting in the family room reading when I came in with a sheaf of papers in my hand. I must have had a look on my face that betrayed my excitement.

"What have you been up to?" she asked with a laugh. "You've been on the phone and have that look that says you know something I don't know."

"How'd you like to move back to California?" I asked, expecting Fay to catch the excitement of the idea.

Instead of brightening up, Fay grew serious and tense; her face showed no expression. "What are you talking about?" she asked.

I unfolded my plan, totally unprepared for the response I was about to get. In the conversation that followed, Fay managed to cut the dream to ribbons.

"How do you know that we'll be able to get licensed?" Fay asked.

"According to both counties we shouldn't have any trouble with my credentials and these plans," I replied.

"But you know how real estate is in southern California. It would cost an arm and a leg!"

"Maybe, but I'm sure we could find something we could afford."

"What about insurance? I'd sure hate to get involved in a lawsuit. That's a big responsibility—taking care of someone else's kids, especially troubled kids."

I began to feel irritated. "What's all this cold water you're throwing on the idea?"

Fay, defensively: "I'm not throwing cold water on your idea. It's just that there are so many questions that need to be answered. Where are you going to get the money?"

"I don't think I'll have any problem getting backers." My irritation grew. It sounded like the same song, second verse.

"But you don't really know. And if you do find backers, you'll have them telling you how to run the home. Are you going to be able to handle that?"

By now I was doing a slow boil. "Wait a minute. What's going on here? You're not listening to what I'm saying. You're shooting me down every time I open my mouth. I've never seen you so negative about this idea. We've talked about it before, and you're usually open! What's going on?"

*The Real Issue.* Fay was quiet and thoughtful. "What *is* going on," she thought out loud. "Why *am* I being so negative?" She began to understand that her potshots at my idea was a defense. The issue wasn't real estate, money, license, insurance, and all the other things we had been kicking around for half an hour.

Finally she said, "I guess I was surprised when you sprang the idea on me. Steven and Dave are on their own, and Pete will be leaving soon for the Navy. Jon will be out of high school in four years. I thought we had decided we wouldn't get tied down to anything like this, but would have a lot of time together, by ourselves, when the boys are gone."

"It's true," I thought. "We did talk about our freedom when all the boys are out of the nest."

As I listened to Fay, I began to realize that we hadn't talked about the idea of a group home for several years, and we had talked about the freedom we'd have when all our kids were gone from home. But I was still irritated because of the way Fay reacted to my idea. Instead of telling me that she had changed her mind about the group home, I felt that she had attacked my idea—no, she had attacked *me*.

Finally I said to Fay, "Why didn't you say that was the problem? I wasn't going to drag you off to California to mother a horde of troubled boys. It was just something we had talked about, and I thought I'd kick it around again with you."

I really began to feel irritated: "Instead of having my idea shot down, I wish I had known at the beginning what the real issue was. It sure would have saved me a lot of aggravation."

"Well, I really didn't know what the problem was when we got started." Fay sounded apologetic. "All I know was that I didn't like the idea, but I didn't know why. So I guess I threw up the road-blocks in self-defense."

I was still irritated in spite of Fay's apologetic tone. "This happens a lot when we talk with each other. I'll get enthusiastic about something, but then I feel I get a bucket of cold water dumped on me!"

"I guess that's what sets me off—the enthusiasm, I

mean," Fay replied. "Sometimes you get so intense I get scared."

*Here We Go Again!* I felt as if she had clubbed me with a baseball bat. "Enthusiasm! Intensity!" How many times over the past twenty-seven years had I heard these words, and how many times had my enthusiasm and intensity been the catalyst of a conflict with Fay?

We married each other because we were different. But neither of us had counted on the things we married for being the very things that would form the core of every conflict.

Fay once put it this way: "I see us as two people at the beach. I test the water with my toe. If it feels okay, I go a little deeper—maybe. You rush in all at once. I feel this is why I don't do some things—I can't get wet all at once. I need to test the water. So rather than feel pushed, I don't do it at all." Once again I was rushing, and Fay was holding back.

I put my head in my hands. The despair was frightening. I couldn't hold back the tears: "After twenty-seven years we're back to square one. When is it going to end? It seems every time I get excited about something I get shot down. Sometimes I feel as if I have a millstone around my neck! It doesn't matter what the issue is; the conflict is the same. My intensity frightens you!"

*Two Very Different People.* We were silent for a long time. Finally Fay spoke. "I wish I knew what to say." Tears welled up in her eyes. "I didn't mean to put you through all that."

"No. It's not the hassle that has me down. It's just that it's the same old conflict."

Fay attempted to be comforting, but I couldn't be reached. I had realized something about us that I hadn't seen before—how different we are in our approach to life. I guess I had known it for a long time, but this was the first time I began to get a clear focus on it—how I boom ahead and how Fay holds back. The realization was devastating.

But it was not just our differentness that had me down. If after twenty-seven years we still pushed and pulled against each other, creating a stir of negative emotions, would it ever end? For two days I couldn't be reached.

Finally I said to Fay, "Please don't think I'm trying to punish you with the 'silent treatment.' I'm just having a rough time climbing out of the hole."

I did climb out of the hole after three or four days with some new insight into our communication problems. But it was not until a year later that I understood clearly what had happened.

*Epilogue.* There was still something about this incident that bothered me, but I didn't know what. I felt that the intensity of my emotions was much greater than warranted by the conflict as I understood it.

As I write this, the snow is falling again. The events of the past year, and particularly those of the past few days, have answered the nagging question about what else was bothering me concerning this incident.

A few days ago Fay and I were preparing to leave our Maryland home for a long weekend at our Virginia home. We are looking forward to the coming of spring, and one of the things we want to do is take our gas-fired outdoor grill to Virginia. It carries a bottle of liquid propane gas (LP), and Fay, being a cautious person, is uneasy about carrying the bottle in the car.

She expressed this concern, so I suggested that since we were taking two cars I drive the one with the LP bottle. But she was just as uneasy with my doing it. The conversation stopped there. I thought, "If I don't take it and she doesn't take it, how will we get it there?" I knew by experience that she wasn't ready to solve the problem then. So I temporarily dropped it.

The next day it snowed, and when I asked Fay what she wanted to do about taking the grill to Virginia, she said that there was snow on the ground, and it would be too much of a hassle to get it into our van.

I said, "I don't mind. It's no trouble."

Fay replied, "I don't want snow tracked in the van. Besides, we can't use it this weekend anyway. Snow is in the forecast again."

I started to do a slow burn and felt exactly as I did over the conversation about the group home. But this time I knew what was bothering me: "She's not being honest with me. It's not the snow or the mess or that we can't use the grill this weekend. She just doesn't want to see that LP bottle carried in the van!"

The time wasn't right to talk about it then, but I decided I had to talk about this when we got to Virginia. I didn't push to take the gas grill.

The day after we got to Virginia we were sitting in front of the fireplace talking, and I brought up the subject. We were talking about this book, and I said, "Something new dawned on me about the incident I relate concerning the group home. It was not just the problem with my intensity that bothered me. Something else dawned on me yesterday."

I then recounted our discussion about the gas grill. "You know," I said, "the thing that bothered me about that discussion was that you gave me all kinds of reasons for not bringing the gas grill. But they were not the real reason. You were just plain nervous about carrying LP in the car."

Fay looked troubled. "You're right. I was afraid, and when I told you, it didn't seem to matter. So I figured I had to come up with better reasons. You're right, they weren't the real reasons, but the real reason wasn't good enough for you."

She then started to cry. (We cry a lot when we talk!) "I always feel I have to defend my position when I talk to you."

She was right. In my usual intense way I wanted to bore ahead and get a solution. But Fay was not ready to talk about alternatives or a solution. Though it was painful, I discovered yet another effect of my intensity on our relationship and how it interacts with Fay's more measured pace. I want a solution *now;* Fay wants some time to think about it. She tries to buy time for herself by giving me more reasons why she feels as she does.

Practically every conflict has the same common denominator: our differentness. Each approaches life with an entirely different attitude: Fay with caution, and I with abandon. I plunge ahead and Fay holds back. This sets up a pattern of negative reinforcement. Fay holds back harder to restrain my enthusiasm. I push all the harder to overcome Fay's restraint.

To keep from getting swept up in my maelstrom, Fay throws up verbal and non-verbal roadblocks to let me know why something is not feasible, practical, practicable, safe, courteous, nice, kind, decent, appropriate, moral, or thoughtful. But the issue really is her *fear*—fear of being dragged along at a pace that she can't take, or fear of exposure to people or circumstances that might threaten her sense of well-being. And for my part the issue is having my enthusiasm dampened and my energy drained off by "unnecessary" caution or fears.

At the root of our communication problem is our differentness. But we have begun to understand what it means to live together as different people and to respect that differentness. We are beginning to understand that the respect for each other's differentness is basic to effective communication in marriage.

In the chapters that follow we address this issue of differentness and how we can avoid letting our differentness interfere with good communication. This can be accomplished by understanding the magnitude of our differentness, respecting it, and accepting it.

# 3

# *We're So Different*

## —BY FAY

WHEN I MARRIED ANDY I was vaguely aware that I married him because I saw qualities that I didn't have—qualities that would make my life richer. And I felt that I had something special to bring to the relationship too. But I never dreamed we were so different! Consider the following items:

- What people think—I tend to be more concerned over what people think than Andy.
- Optimism—Andy tends to be more optimistic than I. My pessimism is my protection. It keeps me from rushing into situations that may be uncomfortable or threatening to me.
- Interests and activities—Andy tends to have more interests and activities than I. The unfamiliar tends to make me hold back and be more cautious.
- Physical activity—I am less physically active than Andy. I am content to stay in the house and read, but he gets the jitters if he can't get out and engage in vigorous physical activity.
- Reading—I read a lot of fiction for entertainment. Andy feels he must read to "better his mind," so he tends to stay with non-fiction.

● Climate and temperature—I find it difficult to take extremes
in climate and temperature. Humidity, heat, wind, and cold
are distressing. Andy has a greater tolerance. This difference
contributes to my being an indoor person and he an outdoor
person.

● Private versus public—I tend to be a more private person
than Andy. I tend to keep to myself what I think, feel, and do.
Andy tends to disclose these things to others more than I.

● Following and leading—I prefer to follow. Andy likes to lead.

● Rules—I'm a stickler for rules. For example, I enter at en-
trance signs and exit at exit signs. Andy will—if it's convenient
for him to do so.

● Communication style—I tend to blurt out to Andy how I
feel. He tends to play it safe and thinks what he's going to say
first and how it will sound.

● Self-expression—I don't feel I can express myself as well as
Andy. He also tends to talk louder and is more verbal. This
used to intimidate me, but we're getting better at this. I'm
talking more; Andy is speaking softer and is less forceful.

● Self-worth—Andy generally feels very good about himself. I
feel better about myself than I used to feel. But I still have a
way to go.

*In The Beginning It Was Not So.* As I listed our differences it
was a painful reminder. I was not always the pessimistic,
dependent follower I turned out to be.

As a teen-ager and young adult I was a leader. When my
best girl friend and I did things together, usually it was I who
suggested things to do. The same was true when my fiancé
and I dated.

I was always an officer in my church group—planning
and leading group activities. Yes, I was soft-spoken and con-
genial. But I wasn't fearful and withdrawn. I didn't suffer
from feelings of low self-worth.

The first blow to my self-worth came when I was nine-
teen. My fiancé broke off our engagement. We had dated
steadily through high school and had been engaged three
months. The pain of that experience made me doubt

myself—"Maybe I'm not the person I thought I was."

The second blow came after I met Andy and was introduced to an entirely different kind of Christian fellowship, where movies were wrong, going to places that served liquor was wrong, smoking was wrong, dancing was wrong—although heavy petting was right! But I went along with it.

After I married Andy he went to college in the Northeast, and the cultural shock blew my mind. I was used to slow southern living with a friendly "Howdy," even from passers-by. Now I was in a fast, intense eastern culture where people seemed to frown all the time and were unfriendly. Store clerks and apartment managers were unbelievably impolite. I felt that something was wrong with me. I just didn't fit in. I was *different,* and that didn't feel good at all.

Then a new set of Christian rules and expectations were imposed on me. If you're a Christian you don't wear make-up. And when I didn't have a favorite Bible verse to quote in prayer meeting at church I was embarrassed and humiliated. I just didn't measure up!

I kept going along with the game plan. By now I was so unsure of myself and felt so unspiritual that I didn't dare voice the feeling of conflict in me—conflict with the past and present and what I felt was right for *me.*

Andy complicated matters further. He always was so sure of himself. I sometimes felt that I needed a battery of lawyers in order to communicate with him. He was right—*always.* His compulsiveness, intensity, and drive often left me in the dust. Even if I did dare open my mouth, I usually was bulldozed.

When Andy was a Christian and Missionary Alliance pastor in Arlington, Virginia, he had a dear District Superintendent, C. J. Mason, who would tell me in Andy's presence, "Hang on to his coattails!" C. J. and I knew what he meant, but it was years before Andy understood that C. J. saw him as a compulsive person.

These memories are painful to recall, but I don't write with bitterness. I relate them only because I want to make an

important point about *differentness*. You cannot communicate
if you feel that your differentness is bad and you feel
rejected—even down to your Texas accent. And I'm sure that
I'm writing to others who have experienced the same thing.
Let me encourage you. Maybe you are different. But don't
cave in! Okay, so you're not where you *ought* to be (how I hate
that word). But that doesn't mean that you're unacceptable
because you're different.

  *The Way Back.* Do you ever get tired of being told you're
wrong? Ever get tired of feeling rotten because you're "different"? Ever get sick of having to comply without any voice in
the matter? Good! There's hope.
  In 1968 Andy accepted a call to a church in southern
California. We all felt it was a good move—except for our
oldest son, Steve, who then was in the ninth grade. As it
turned out, he loved California and is still there.
  But once again I found myself in a very intense situation,
over which I had no control. I was expected to go along with
the game plan once more. By now I was tired of being com-
pelled to do things without having any voice in the matter. I
did a lot of soul searching. What did *I* feel about my marriage? What did *I* feel about the power struggles and politics
in the church? What were *my* personal convictions? It was
then I began to set my own pace.
  As Providence would have it, God came down hard on
Andy at the same time. While he was taking further training
in marriage and family counseling he was required to have
encounter group experiences. The groups finally got to him.
They helped him see what I had been saying for years about
his intense, compulsive, dominating ways.
  God decided it was time for a change in the game plan.
While Andy was being encouraged to back off, I was being
encouraged to speak my mind. It wasn't easy for us, but it was
a start.
  In 1973 we left California to go back to the Washington

D.C. area where Andy set up a marriage and family counseling practice. We had an opportunity for a new start as private citizens once again.

These have been good years of growth—not without pain. But we have a handle on the basic problem that kept us apart for years—our differentness.

*Opposites Do Attract.* Differentness is not a bad thing so long as it is not as extreme as ours once was. In fact, psychologists describe the attraction of opposites as a "complementary relationship." Two people exchange different types of behavior. One gives and the other receives. This type of relationship is more workable in marriage than the symmetrical relationship. In this kind of relationship both tend to be alike and competitive. If the wife points out that she has succeeded in some endeavor, the husband points out that he has succeeded in an equally important endeavor.[1]

In a complementary relationship it is important, however, that each brings something into the relationship and that each takes a turn at being teacher and pupil. Early in our relationship this was not so. Andy was always the teacher, and I was always the pupil. Even though I had something to offer the relationship out of my differentness, Andy's way usually prevailed. Being more verbal and forceful, he was able to make his way stick.

But I am to blame also. I conspired by giving in. As I have said already, I grew to doubt my own opinions and feelings. I wasn't as sure of myself as he was.

I'm beginning to recapture the good things I liked about myself in my youth. I will always be soft-spoken, but now I can be soft-spoken and expect my opinions and feelings to be respected—*because my differentness* is now respected by both Andy and me.

*The Mathematics of Marriage.* Christians tend to view the mathematics of marriage as $1 + 1 = 1$. They feel that becoming "one flesh" means being totally absorbed by each other.

The Biblical reference to "one flesh" (Gen. 2:24) has reference to sexual union and not the obliteration of all differences. The proper mathematics of marriage is $1 + 1 = 3$. We are two individuals and a couple. As healthy individuals, we each bring to the marriage something different and unique.

*Summary.* Since most couples marry for complementary reasons, they will be required to harmonize their differences. Andy and I have found this possible by observing a cardinal principle of communication: My position is not *better than* but *different from* yours.

# 4

# *Acceptance: The Bottom Line*

## —BY ANDRÉ

AS A HIGHLY OPINIONATED PERSON, I have had a great deal of difficulty accepting a person who holds a different point of view than mine. And worse, as a Bible-believing Christian I have used the Bible not only to support my view but also to club the other person into submission. For many years my attitude was, "If God's Word says it, you believe it and do it whether or not you like it."

Someone may ask, "What's wrong with that?" The thing wrong was my attitude. I could not separate the person from his opinion. I could not accept the person if his opinions differed from mine.

God has come down hard on me for my lack of acceptance. Twelve years ago when I was a pastor I gradually was made aware of my unloving dogmatism, which made me a very unaccepting person. Even Fay suffered from it. I remember being shaken by something I read while preaching through the Book of First Peter. In 2:17 the Greek text reads literally, "Honor all men! Keep loving the brotherhood, keep fearing God, keep honoring the king." Evidently the Christians to whom Peter writes were loving the brotherhood (other Christians). They were fearing God and honoring the king. Peter says, "Keep it up, but do one more thing. Honor *all* men."

The word *honor* (timaō) means "to recognize the worth of something." Peter is asking us to recognize the worth of all human beings. According to Genesis 9:6, human beings are of great worth because they are made in the image of God—yes, even unregenerate men are made in the image of God. The fall did not efface the image.

Opinionated, dogmatic people are the world's worst at accepting other people as creatures worthy of honor. Christ and the Pharisees illustrate this difference. When Christ ate with publicans and sinners he was not approving of their sinfulness, but He did make them feel accepted as people. Feeling accepted, they were ready to listen to what Jesus said. The Pharisees withdrew from the sinners.

### THE IMPORTANCE OF ACCEPTANCE

One of the skills essential to counseling is "non-possessive warmth." This is an attitude of acceptance that says, "You don't have to agree with me in order for me to accept your worth as a human being and to share my warmth with you." This skill must be learned not only by counselors but by all who would communicate effectively.[1]

This does not mean that you surrender your own point of view. It means that you care enough about the other person not to bludgeon him into accepting your point of view. This is why it's called *nonpossessive* warmth. Your warmth toward that person is not conditioned on his agreeing with you. This is why some psychologists call the attitude "unconditional positive regard."

*God's Acceptance.* The finest example of this is God's attitude of acceptance toward us. The Bible declares that while we were yet *sinners* God reached out in love and sent His son to die for our sins (Rom. 5:8). He didn't wait for us to agree with Him before He showed His care for us.

Acceptance doesn't mean you never question the other person's behavior. It means that his *worth* is not questioned.

*George and Ella.* George is a devout Christian and a serious student of the Bible.

He sought marriage counseling because, according to him, his wife, Ella, was not being a submissive Christian wife. He made it clear that he expected me as a Christian counselor to convince her of her disobedience.

George was rigid and unloving. He was giving Ella the clear message that she was a bad person because she was not submissive to him.

When I pointed out to George how harsh and unloving he was, he became indignant. The very idea that I should find anything wrong with *him!* He wasn't the disobedient one. It was his wife. How dare I suggest that there might be a problem with him?

What was happening here? George did not understand unconditional positive regard. His regard for his wife was indeed conditional. The only way she would find any positive regard or acceptance from him would be to see things exactly as he did and do exactly as he said.

Needless to say, Ella's self-worth took a beating at George's hands. And by this attitude George guaranteed Ella's resistance. She wasn't going to let him completely destroy her self-worth. She just dug in her heels and resisted him with all she had.

If George had accepted Ella, he would have boosted her feeling of self-worth. And out of those good feelings of self-worth she would have been more willing to consider George's point of view. By not forcing Ella, George would have found her more willing to give. We often give freely what we do not permit a person to take by force.

ACCEPTANCE OF FEELINGS

Acceptance is not just a philosophical or mental exercise, however. It sounds noble to say, "I accept this human being's worth." It goes deeper than that. It respects his *feelings*.

*Feeling Versus Fact.* Many couples make the mistake of trying to establish who's right and who's wrong. They attempt to establish what the *facts* are and the *right course of action* based on those facts. Now that is reasonable enough—if you are in a court of law with rules of evidence, a judge, jury, lawyers, and appeals procedure. But an adversary proceeding—which this is—is unworkable in marriage. We don't have the machinery in marriage to communicate and solve our problems this way. Strangely enough, in marital communication we really can't start with the facts!

How many times have you been frustrated in your attempt to communicate on the basis of fact? The wife says, "Now the facts are . . ." But the husband says, "No they're not! You have the facts all wrong. The facts are . . ."

*The Real Issues.* The real issues are these: 1) how do I *feel* about this? 2) are you willing to respect my *feelings?* 3) how do you *feel* about this? 4) am I willing to respect your *feelings?* Here we get back to the cardinal rule of communication: *My position is not better than, but different from, yours.*

Now remember, I am applying this only to marital communication. In a court of law we can be interested in the facts. When we go to church, we are interested in an authoritative opinion from the preacher.

But the relationship between husband and wife is different. It is supposed to be a relationship of mutual acceptance and respect. We are not attempting to find out what the facts are. We are trying to discover how each feels. Once we understand where we are in relation to each other we can decide what we want to do about our differences. We are in a position of compromising, or agreeing to disagree. If we can't do either, we can go to court and let someone else decide who's right and who has the facts. That's called divorce!

As a Christian marriage and family counselor I often find that facts do have a bearing on the cases I handle. And I often must address those facts in the light of Scripture because my authoritative point of view is being sought. But in my relationship with Fay I cannot be the authority. If she wants to put me in that position, inadvisable as it might be, that's her choice. I don't force it on her. But our relationship is that of husband and wife and not preacher and parishioner, counselor and client.

*Keep Off the Grass!* I was having difficulty getting my boat trailer turned around in order to back into my driveway. So I decided I would pull up a few feet on the lot next to my neighbor's house to make my turn. Fay, who was riding with me, stiffened and asked, "What are you doing?"

"Turning around," I answered.

"On Bill's grass?"

I really didn't think Bill would mind, but I did know that Fay *felt* that Bill would mind, and she reacted accordingly. So I backed up and made my turn without driving on Bill's grass. It was more difficult, but I was willing to go the more difficult route out of respect for her feelings. Because I love her, her feelings were more important than right or wrong.

The next day I had the boat out again, but this time Fay wasn't with me. But I still respected her feelings and stayed off Bill's grass when I brought the boat home. As I was getting out of my van, Bill came over and asked, "Why didn't you pull up on the grass to make your turn? It would be easier that way."

I must admit I felt smug. And it did cross my mind to tell Fay that *I was right!* But what would that accomplish, except to identify myself as her adversary and encourage her to start keeping score when she is right?

It cost me very little to respect her feelings—and to continue to respect her feelings. I want her to know that she doesn't have to think and feel as I do in order to be okay in my eyes.

Saying that I felt smug may come across as a put-down of Fay. Hadn't Bill said it was okay? Wouldn't Fay then feel it was okay? It's not a matter of who's right, but of the right thing to do, isn't it?

That would be true, except for a further complication. Over the years I had damaged our relationship by always trying to prove I was right. If I opened the issue again, it might have appeared to Fay that I was trying to prove I was right.

If *Bill* had told Fay it was all right to drive on his grass, there would have been no problem. She would have been free to decide what she wanted us to do in light of that new information. But if *I* told her what Bill had said, it might have sounded as if I couldn't let the matter drop. It would have sounded as if I had to be right.

Now I know that Bill volunteered the information and that I would only have been passing it on. But given the history of my bad behavior, it was far better to drop the matter and not appear as though I was trying to prove I was right.

*Owning the Problem.* I have been stressing the acceptance of the *person*. Quite apart from his behavior, this person has worth. But what happens when he behaves in a way that jeopardizes my sense of security and well-being?

For example, a husband may grant that his wife is a creature made in God's image and is worthwhile. But her flirtatiousness with other men may make him feel insecure. He has in marriage established a strong emotional bond with her, but now he feels that it is jeopardized by her *behavior*.

Rather than tell her what a bad person she is, he would do better to own the problem *as his*.

By "owning the problem" I mean this. He is to approach her with the idea that the problem between them is not due to the fact that she is a bad or morally defective person. He cannot establish himself as the authority in the relationship and sit as judge on her behavior.

But he can report *his feelings* about the problem. By reporting his feelings he "owns the problem." He accepts responsibility for finding a problem with what's going on. When he sees her act overly friendly *he feels insecure* and *fearful* for the marriage.

Ultimately, she may see her behavior as a problem and may accept the responsibility to change. But it cannot be forced on her. By calling attention to the problem without condemning the other person we are able to address the problem without alienating that person.

I'll have more to say about this later. But I must point this out here so as not to leave the impression that I think all behavior is relative and that anything goes in marriage. Indeed, it does not.

When the woman caught in adultery was dragged before Jesus, his attitude was non-condemning toward her. But he did say, "Go and sin no more" (John 8:11).

## WATCH OUT FOR THESE

Non-accepting spouses tend to fall into one of four categories. They are similar in that they ignore feelings and stress fact, but their emphasis differs.

*Lawyers.* Lawyers want to build a *case*. If necessary they will call in *witnesses* to corroborate the *facts*. They are masters at *cross-examining* and discrediting the spouse's case.

*Bible Thumpers.* Bible Thumpers are the religious counterpart of lawyers. They use the *authority of Scripture* to support their position and quote *chapter and verse*. Differences with the spouse are met with the *preaching of the truth*. Their byword is, "It doesn't matter how you feel. If God's Word says it, we are to do it."

*Fact Finders.* Fact Finders may be religious or irreligious. They pride themselves in having a good *memory* and *recall* of the *facts*. They pride themselves in being *logical, unemotional* people who don't let feelings cloud the *issues*. Clerks, accountants and others who have an eye for *detail* make good Fact Finders.

*King James.* King James doesn't have to build a case like the lawyer. He may not quote the Bible. Logic and memory may not be his forte. King James always has *"The Authorized Version,"* and his version is to be accepted because he is king!

*Summary.* The all-important question I'm attempting to answer here is this: "Can we live together in a spirit of good will, respecting each other's feelings?" Others may be able to bring the facts to bear on our situation—doctors, lawyers, and marriage counselors. And sometimes we must resort to outside authority. But the day-to-day conflicts we must solve are too numerous and usually too insignificant to be solved by appeal to authority. They are most readily solved in a spirit of good will where we accept each other and respect each other's feelings.

# Rating Your Spouse's Acceptance

## —By Fay

HOW ACCEPTED DOES your spouse make you feel? Sixteen rating statements below are provided for your evaluation. You are to answer how *you* feel. For example, in response to number one, do you or don't you feel guilty when you ask for things or want your way? You need not defend or justify your answer. Just be honest about the way you feel. When you are done, you will have an opportunity to explain why you feel as you do.

*How To Rate Your Spouse.* You will see that each statement has three choices: no, mid, and yes. If you cannot answer yes or no, you may use the mid. But use the yes and no responses as much as you can.

Take a sheet of paper and number it from one to sixteen. When you respond to each statement, use the number from the appropriate column. For example, if the answer is "no" write down the number you see in the "no" column, even though it is sometimes three and sometimes one. Both hus-

band and wife should fill out a rating sheet and evaluate each
other without consultation. Be sure that you respond to each
statement.

RATE YOUR SPOUSE'S ACCEPTANCE

|  | NO | MID | YES |
|---|---|---|---|
| 1) I feel guilty when I ask for things or sometimes want my way. | 3 | 2 | 1 |
| 2) I am afraid of making mistakes around him/her. | 3 | 2 | 1 |
| 3) I feel it necessary to defend my actions when I'm with him/her. | 3 | 2 | 1 |
| 4) I am bothered by fears of feeling stupid or inadequate with him/her. | 3 | 2 | 1 |
| 5) Criticism from him/her hurts my feelings of worth. | 3 | 2 | 1 |
| 6) I feel free to show my weaknesses in front of him/her. | 1 | 2 | 3 |
| 7) I can care for myself in spite of his/her feelings for me. | 1 | 2 | 3 |
| 8) I am afraid to be myself with him/her. | 3 | 2 | 1 |
| 9) I feel free to express my needs to him/her. | 1 | 2 | 3 |
| 10) I find that I must give him/her reasons for my feelings. | 3 | 2 | 1 |
| 11) I can be negative or positive with him/her. | 1 | 2 | 3 |
| 12) My wants, likes, dislikes, and values are respected by him/her. | 1 | 2 | 3 |

|     |                                                      |   |   |   |
|-----|------------------------------------------------------|---|---|---|
| 13) | I sometimes ask for my needs to be met.              | 1 | 2 | 3 |
| 14) | I can be inconsistent or illogical with him/her.     | 3 | 2 | 1 |
| 15) | I am afraid to show my fears to him/her.             | 3 | 2 | 1 |
| 16) | I am afraid to show tears in front of him/her.       | 3 | 2 | 1 |

*Scoring.* After you have responded to each statement, add up your score. The highest possible score is 48; the lowest score is 16.

Remember, you are rating your spouse by saying how accepted *you feel.* Let's rate as follows:

| 40-48 | Strong feelings of acceptance |
| 32-39 | Lack some feeling of acceptance |
| 24-31 | Serious feelings of unacceptance |
| 16-23 | Your communication needs lots of work. |

*Evaluation of the Questions.* After you have rated your spouse, go back to the rating statements and look at each response. Several of the statements are similar and probe the same area of self-worth. They are worded differently to approach it from many angles. I'll consider each statement separately, however, so you can locate the ones you are especially interested in talking about.

1) "I feel guilty when I ask for things or sometimes want my way." The ideal answer is "no." If your spouse accepts you it means that you should be able to ask for what you want, or ask for your way, without feeling guilty. Equality in marriage means give and take. Ephesians 5:28–29 and First Peter 3:7 teach equality of the spouses as "fellow-heirs of the grace of God."

If you do feel guilty, be sure it's not a lack of self-acceptance. Sometimes people are raised with the idea that they should not ask anything for themselves. Here the problem is lack of self-acceptance, which may or may not be aggravated by the spouse.

2) "I am afraid of making mistakes around him/her." The ideal answer is "no." In an accepting relationship your mistakes are not thrown in your face. This is the spirit of First Corinthians 13. Love is longsuffering and kind. So is acceptance.

A "yes" answer may indicate the likelihood of ridicule for mistakes, or it may indicate impatience. Sometimes it's verbal and other times non-verbal. A disgusted look, a sigh with eyes rolling is enough to give the message, "I can't accept you that way—you dummy."

There's always the possibility, on the other hand, of making "mistakes" on purpose so you can make the other person lose his cool.

3) "I feel it necessary to defend my actions when I'm with him/her." The ideal answer is "no."

Gross or sinful behavior ought to be questioned. But when practically all of your actions are called into question, your spouse is giving the message that you can't do anything right. The message is that your entire approach to life is wrong. It is another way of saying, "Do it my way and you'll be right."

Usually your spouse's actions are not better or worse than yours. They are just different. Remember, *not better than, but different from.*

4) "I am bothered by fears of feeling stupid or inadequate with him/her." The ideal answer is "no."

An accepting attitude builds the other person's confidence. It believes in the other person. Again, the spirit of First Corinthians 13: Love "bears all things, believes all things, hopes all things, endures all things" (v. 7).

I'm not advocating naïve optimism. What I say here should be balanced by an understanding of people who don't want to communicate. What I'm saying here relates to normal, healthy people who want to communicate and make the relationship work.

5) "Criticism from him/her hurts my feelings of worth." The ideal answer is "no."

This doesn't mean we never criticize. How we go about it is another matter. The criticism should be gentle, constructive, and indirect—in the form of an "I" message, which is discussed later in this book. Criticism is given in the spirit of Galatians 6:1.

A "yes" answer may not indicate the fault is entirely in a critical partner. A person who is overly sensitive to criticism may feel criticism when it's not really there. A fragile ego tends to see criticism everywhere.

6) "I feel free to show my weaknesses in front of him/her." The ideal answer is "yes."

This is a variation on statements 2 and 4. Mistakes, stupidity, inadequacy, and weaknessess are all issues that come up in a relationship.

A "no" answer may not necessarily indicate unacceptance, however. Often when I ask a husband this question he will say, "Yes, I'm afraid to show my weakness to my wife. But it doesn't have anything to do with her. I can't show my weakness to anyone. A man ought to be strong and have his act together."

7) "I can care for myself in spite of his/her feelings for me." The ideal answer is "yes."

It's unrealistic to expect the unflinching approval of your spouse at all times. But the spouse's lack of approval should not exceed your ability to like yourself anyway.

8) "I am afraid to be myself with him/her." The ideal answer is "no."

One's self-identity is very important in marriage. Can I be me and still be accepted by you?

Again, we're not dealing with sinful or gross behavior here. I once heard a woman-chasing-man tell his wife, "That's

the way I am. I have to be true to my own needs." Her reply
was, "I have to be true to myself too, so I guess it's good-by."

9) "I feel free to express my needs." The ideal answer is
"yes." This is a variation on statement 1. Refer to my comments there.

10) "I find that I must give reasons for my feelings." The
ideal answer is "no."

Whether or not we *should* feel as we do, a comfortable
relation depends on acceptance in spite of those feelings. Identifying and reporting those feelings is the first step to doing
something about them. If I am unaccepted because of the way
I feel, it's unlikely that my feelings will change. I will just
create distance from you.

11) "I can be negative or positive with him/her." The
ideal answer is "yes."

Acceptance means that I can take a position different
from yours and still be okay. Some marriages suffer from a
"chameleon syndrome." One spouse continually takes on the
color of the other to avoid conflict. This kind of marriage is in
danger because they never talk about their differences.

12) "My wants, likes, dislikes, and values are respected
by him/her." The ideal answer is "yes."

Here we have a variation on the chameleon syndrome
mentioned in statement 11. Your wants, likes, dislikes, and
values need not be colored the same as mine in order for you to
be accepted by me.

Again, we're not dealing with sinful or gross behavior or
with a value system. Generally, the value system of each
spouse is the same. It's the particulars in that system we have
problems with. We may be committed to going to church, but
whether or not we miss a Sunday for a particular reason will
reveal our differentness. For example, you may not feel like
attending church when you're traveling. But I may think we
should go to church whether we're at home or on the road.

13) "I sometimes ask for my needs to be met." The ideal
answer is "yes."

This is a variation on statement 1. See that statement for comment.

14) "I can be inconsistent or illogical with him/her." The ideal answer is "yes."

This is a variation on statements 3 and 10. Remember, acceptance means that we avoid being a lawyer and building a case. Total consistency and logic are not essential to good communication. But at least some consistency or some logic is necessary.

Sometimes, to avoid being pinned down, people will continually change their position. Here we get into sick communication, which we deal with later in the book.

15) "I am afraid to show my fears to him/her." The ideal answer is "no."

Fear is a special type of feeling. Can I feel the way I do and still be okay in your eyes?

Sometimes fears are not revealed for another reason. Often Andy avoids expressing his fears to me simply because he doesn't want to alarm me! He thinks that if he tells me his fears I'll become more fearful than necessary. It doesn't make for good communication, I know. But he sees me as a worrier, and he doesn't want to aggravate my tendency to worry.

16) "I am afraid to show my tears in front of him/her." The ideal answer is "no."

This is a variation on statement 6 (weakness) and 15 (fears). See these statements for comment.

*Summary.* The purpose of this rating exercise is to give each spouse an idea of how accepted the other feels. After you have completed your rating sheets, sit down and go over the responses with each other. You may go through all the responses one sheet at a time or you may want to compare how you each responded item by item. But be careful how you respond to the other's rating. If your spouse reports feelings of unacceptance, be careful of your response. Don't say, "You shouldn't feel that way." If you do say that, you will have missed the point and will reveal the basic flaw in your communication style. Whether or not *you* think your spouse's evaluation is correct, that's how your spouse feels. Don't fall into the role of being Lawyer, Bible Thumper, Fact-Finder, or King James.

You must start with how your spouse feels, whether or not you like it. The harmony of the relationship must not depend on your spouse's agreeing with you. It must start with a respect for those feelings.

# 6

# *Are You REALLY Listening?*

## —BY ANDRÉ

FAY AND I ARE GETTING BETTER at listening to each other. In fact, I think we do a pretty good job.

It wasn't always so. We both have had problems listening. The expression on my face and my body language once were very clear signals that I wasn't listening. When Fay would say something I didn't like I'd become fidgety and act as if I were ready to jump in at the first opportunity to give "The Authorized Version." I was thinking of what I wanted to say instead of being attentive to what she was saying.

Fay's style was different. She would withdraw when she didn't like what she heard. I could see the walls going up just by the expression on her face.

### LEARN TO ACTIVE-LISTEN

Every effective communicator must learn the skill of "active-listening." It's called "active" because the listener has a responsibility. He works at grasping what the speaker is saying and attempts to help him express those feelings. This is extremely difficult to do, especially when we hear criticism, or something we disagree with. Our inclination is to tune out or correct what is said. It's foreign to self-preservation to help someone dump a load of painful verbiage on us! But when we do active-listen we convey a clear message of acceptance. Whether or not we agree with what is being said, we convey the message that this person is worth being heard.

*How To Active-Listen.* Just exactly what do we do when we active-listen? We must crawl inside the speaker's skin and see life as he sees it, hear it as he hears it, and feel it as he feels it. All effective counselors have this skill. It's called "accurate empathy."[1] Empathy is a caring attitude that enables us to perceive life the way the speaker perceives it. But it's called *accurate* empathy in that we perceive it *exactly* as that other person perceives it. We neither overshoot nor undershoot.

If someone tells you he's depressed, you need to assess the degree. Is it just something passing, does it border on suicidal urge, or is it a chronic problem that has been wearing on him for weeks?

When you accurately touch that person where he is hurting, that in itself is healing. Often I have had clients brighten up at that moment of contact and say, "You're the first person who really has understood where I am!" A marvelous transaction takes place at that moment when the pain and hurt are shared by the accurately empathic listener.

Many times in marriage, solutions are not necessary. Often, a husband or wife only wants to be heard and understood. Satisfied with that, they will often drop the matter.

We must do several things in active-listening.

1) Listen to both words and feelings. Every message has two components: words and feelings. If we do not tune in to how the feelings qualify the words, we will not have heard accurately. Consider the following:

Husband to wife: "Be sure to have the oil in the car checked every time you get gas."

Now consider it's being said this way:

Husband to wife: "If you keep driving the car without oil, you'll burn out the engine for sure!"

Both of those messages carried essentially the same words: The oil in the car should be checked regularly. But the second message definitely carries a *feeling* of hostility. To ignore the feelings and simply to agree to have the oil checked is to miss an important part of the message. The husband is telling his wife *more* than the words convey. He's telling her he is irritated at the way she treats the car. That message is as important as the message about checking the oil—perhaps *more* important. Cars are fixed easier than marriages!

2) Respond to feelings. The second thing we must do is *respond* to those feelings we hear. And we must do it without attack or defense.

Wife to husband: "I don't know what you're getting huffy about. I usually have the oil checked" (defense). "And anyway, who are you to talk about neglecting the car?" (attack).

The following response would be more constructive:

Wife to husband: "It sounds as if you're irritated over the way I take care of the car."

In the first case, the wife is responding to the feelings of her husband but in a defensive and attacking way. Her response is saying in essence, "You have no right to feel the way you do." Whether or not he *should* feel that way, he *does*. And that's what she needs to deal with. The quickest way to deal constructively with negative feelings *is to make that person feel heard and understood.*

In the second case, the wife is saying, "I hear your irritation, and I want you to know that I'm open to hearing more about it." This may lead to the revelation of lots of other feelings that have been creating a breach between husband and wife.

3) Look for non-verbal cues. We must tune in to all the cues the speaker is giving. What emotion is being revealed by his behavior and the tone of his voice? Is it anger, nervousness,

despair, or what? By tuning into those cues you sometimes will put the speaker in touch with emotions he may not be aware of. For example you can say, "It sounds as if there's a lot of despair in what you say." It gives the speaker an opportunity to listen to what he's saying.

In looking for non-verbal cues, ask yourself what the eyes are saying. Are they downcast, darting about, glaring at you, or warm and friendly? The body—what is it saying? Is it tense or relaxed? The inflection of the voice—what mood does it convey? Is it optimism, anxiety, despair, or what? Does the person talking mumble or speak up?

How we dress and the way we present ourselves when we speak carries a message of how we want people to hear us. The hostile person may be conveying the message, "You better treat me right. I can be mean." The docile person may be saying by that behavior, "Don't hurt me. I'm harmless." Trust your instinct. How does that person affect you? And don't be afraid to relate your experience back in a non-attacking way.

For many years I presented myself as a confident, hard-driving person who was quite immune to having his feelings hurt. The message was, "If you compete with me I'll blow you away. And it doesn't matter how you try to beat me. You can't hurt me." I was really protecting myself by discouraging competition and attack. But when I really did hurt and wanted comfort, no one could believe I really needed it. I made my non-verbal cues of confidence that believable!

4) Give adequate feedback. Active-listening requires adequate feedback. When we listen we are not to absorb passively. We are to respond in such a way as to let that person know we have accurately heard. Use various forms of feedback:

    a) I see, you are saying . . .
    b) Let me see if I understand you correctly . . .
    c) Help me to understand; you mean . . .
    d) It sounds as if . . .

e) You find it difficult . . .

f) You are really . . .

g) It's kind of like . . .

h) So you are saying . . .[2]

Your feedback should reveal empathy. It should match the mood of the speaker. A deadpan, mechanical response does not reveal empathy. Active listening is not a gimmick. You must be able to feel what the speaker feels, and let him know that you feel it in a believable way.

5) Words are not the only vehicle for the communication of understanding. The following non-verbal clues aid in creating an atmosphere of acceptance and an attitude of listening:

a) Eye contact

b) Nodding

c) Body expression

d) Facial expression

6) Listed below are appropriate and useful verbal expressions that are effective in facilitating active-listening:

a) Simple acknowledgment—Uh-huh; oh, yeah; and so on.

b) Paraphrase—re-statement of main idea or feelings in your own words. Indicates your receptiveness and understanding of the message.

c) Door openers—"I'd like to hear more about it." "Would you like to talk about it?"

d) Summarize—briefly recap and synthesize what you thought you heard.

e) Seeking information—without introducing new topics or going off on a tangent, ask for confirmation. Check perceptions: "From what I'm hearing, it seems you feel that . . . Am I right?"

f) Ask for elaboration, expansion—"Can you give me an example?"

g) Ask for definition (of words introduced by sender) —"What's a . . . ?" "Who's . . . ?"[3]

WHAT WE ACHIEVE BY ACTIVE-LISTENING

Active-listening is the practical application of acceptance (see chapter 4). It gives the speaker a feeling of acceptance. You have cared enough to stop and hear what he has said, and you care that he feels as he does. It doesn't mean that you have forsaken your own convictions or that you look at things the way he does. But it does mean that you care about him and are able to put yourself in his shoes.

*We Help Others Hear.* When we active-listen, we help that person to hear himself. I remember once unburdening myself to a friend who was active-listening. I said in angry, bitter tones, "I don't care how they feel!" He replied, "You sound hurt and angry." That was true. I was so hurt that I couldn't even tune into where the other people were. I couldn't believe that I actually said I didn't care about them. But that was the truth—hard as it was to face.

*We Reduce the Threat of Criticism.* When we active-listen we reduce the threat of criticism. It's always difficult to tell someone else what's going on inside you because he might criticize. If you want your spouse to talk, don't make him sorry he opened his mouth. By active-listening you will reduce that threat.

*Listening Brings About Change.* I mentioned earlier in the chapter the counseling skill of accurate empathy. This type of caring forms a bond between the speaker and the listener. When the listener touches the speaker where he hurts, an intimate bond of sharing is established. The listener has not judged the speaker, but rather has helped bear the burden.

When this kind of bond is established, the listener is in a much better position to be a positive, changing force in the speaker's life. He is no longer an adversary, but a friend and companion. As such, his life might be a worthwhile model to consider. Listening usually is met with listening in return.

Truax and Carkhuff, writing to counselors in training, speak of this phenomenon. Husbands and wives should have the same therapeutic impact on each other.

> It is in this sense that the therapist, through trial identification, becomes the "other self" or "alter ego" of the client; and through his example leads the patient into a deeper self-exploration and experiencing of feelings and emotional content. As the patient moves tentatively toward feelings and experiences that he experiences as shameful, fearful, or even terrifying, the therapist steps into the patient's shoes and takes him one step further in self-exploration, doing so in a self-accepting and congruent manner that lessens the patient's own fears of coming to grips with the experiences or feelings. It is as if the therapist were providing a model for the patient to follow; as if he were saying by his example, "Even these fearful or terrifying experiences or feelings are not so terrible that they can't be touched and looked at." The therapist's example of self-acceptance and congruence is perhaps as crucial as his ability to sense or at least point to the next step in the patient's self-exploration.[4]

## How To Know When You've Listened

Understanding what another person is saying is really more difficult than it seems. Here are two suggestions that may help you test your listening skills.

*Restate What You Have Heard.* The next time you're involved in a lively discussion that seems to be going nowhere, try this. Restate the other person's position *to his satisfaction* before you proceed to state your own. It must be more than a repetition of words. You should be able to catch the feeling of the words and rephrase them in your own words.[5]

Remember, active-listening requires your active participation in understanding. Try some of the feedback statements mentioned on page 55. Nodding the head and saying, "Yes, I understand," lets the speaker know you're with him. Eye contact is important too. He needs to know you're with him.

*Revolving Discussion Sequence.* When the discussion really is hot and heavy and you need to slow it down, try the Revolving Discussion Sequence. It has three elements: statement, re-statement, and agreement. The statement must be a *feeling* statement, not an opinion.

If you find it difficult to identify feelings, consult the word list on page 96. One cue that lets you know you're going to state an opinion rather than a feeling is the word "that." If you say, "I feel that . . ." you're probably going to give an opinion rather than a feeling. For example, "I feel that you're neglecting me," is not a feeling—it's an opinion. The opinion is that *you* are doing something. And if I accuse you of doing something bad, you're going to defend yourself with an opinion of your own. On the other hand, "I feel neglected" is a statement of feeling that accuses you of nothing. I feel something. Because you are not accused, you will be less likely to challenge the statement.

The statement in the Revolving Discussion Sequence involves a feeling and the reason for the feeling. For example, a husband may say to his wife, "I feel neglected because the children seem to get more of your time than I do."

The wife is to restate his feelings and the reason for it. She will say, "I hear you saying that you feel neglected because it seems that the children get more of my time than you." Or she can put it in her own words. It is important that she restate the husband's statement until he is satisfied that she has heard him.

Then comes the agreement. *She must agree that he feels that way.* She may want to argue that she doesn't spend more time with the children and may want to advance proof of her position. She must not! If she does, she is not listening to his feelings.

The fact of the matter is that he does feel that way, and nothing short of being heard and understood will do. I'm not saying that she cannot have feelings of her own. She will, and her opportunity to express them will come. But this step of the sequence is essential to the whole. Whether or not she thinks her husband *should* feel as he does, the fact of the matter is, that's where he is!

Having completed that stage of the sequence, it's the wife's turn to speak. She may say, "I feel overloaded when I hear all the needs you and the children have."

The husband may be tempted to say, "You shouldn't feel that way. All you have to do is . . ." Suggestions for change are inappropriate at this point. He needs to hear all that she has to say on the subject, and she needs to hear all he has to say. Many times we offer solutions before we fully understand the problem.

After the wife makes her statement, the husband must restate what she has said. He must do it to her satisfaction. She needs to know he has heard her. He must not be impatient in trying to get it right. An attitude of impatience says, "You shouldn't feel that way."

Once the wife is satisfied with the husband's restatement, he then must agree with her. Yes, she does feel overloaded. Whether or not he thinks she should feel overloaded, that's where she is.

And she must know that she can feel that way and still be okay in her husband's eyes. He may want to see some changes in the household routine, but those changes have nothing to do with the okayness of his wife as a person. *Change comes quickest where there is mutual acceptance and respect!*

ERRORS IN ACTIVE-LISTENING

When you practice active-listening you will want to watch out for some common errors.[6]

*Active-Listening When Other Help Is Needed.* Active-listening is inappropriate when other help is needed. When a young mother is distraught trying to diaper a screaming baby and keep her two-year-old off the coffee table at the same time, she doesn't need to be listened to. She needs help!

*Focusing Only on Feelings.* It is important to listen to feelings. But we must not let the feelings get in the way of hearing *why* the person feels as he does.

*Active-Listening When You Don't Have Time.* You and your wife are having breakfast. She feels very blue. Life is uninteresting, and today looks as if it's going to be another dull day. Your car pool leaves in five minutes. Don't try to active-listen then. Call her when you get a chance or set a time to talk that evening.

*Being Too Interpretive.* There's a big difference between making a person feel heard and engaging in psychoanalysis. You may restate with accurate empathy *what* your spouse is feeling, but *why* he feels that way is really his to discover. When we try to focus on *why* people feel as they do, they often think that we're really not interested in *what* they are feeling.

*Feeding Back With No Effect Or Empathy.* A truly caring person shows it in his attitude toward those who reveal their feelings. This is one of the distinguishing characteristics of Jesus Christ, who is "touched with the feeling of our infirmities" (Heb. 4:15 KJV).

*Feeding Back Only Part of the Feeling.* Often, the expression of many feelings add up to a few general feelings. We must stay with the flow of feelings and try to put together an overview of what's happening. The speaker may ramble, but the listener should be able to hear an underlying theme.

*Summary.* Active-listening is a way to convey to the speaker your feeling of acceptance. You may not look at life as he does, and you will want to express your view too. But for the moment, as an active-listener, you are making that person feel that he's worth being heard.

Remember, listening begets listening.

# Rating Your Spouse
# As a Listener

## —By Fay

How does your spouse rate as an active-listener? The rating scale below is provided for your evaluation. How you respond to the statements will help your spouse understand how well he rates in this skill. This rating, as in chapter 5, is not intended to be a scientific instrument. It is an estimate of your spouse's listening skills and will give him an idea of the relative strength and weakness he has as a listener. Your spouse is to rate you also.

Do not consult each other as you are doing the rating. You will have an opportunity to discuss the answers when you are done.

*How To Rate Your Spouse.* Take a sheet of paper and number it from one to sixteen. When you respond to each statement use the number from the appropriate column. If the answer is "no," write down the number you see in the "no" column, even though it is sometimes one and sometimes three. Remember you rate your spouse by how *you feel*.

## Rate Your Spouse As a Listener

| | NO | MID | YES |
|---|---|---|---|
| 1) He/she understands the way I feel. | 1 | 2 | 3 |
| 2) He/she values me as an individual or unique person. | 1 | 2 | 3 |
| 3) He/she feels deeply my most painful feelings. | 1 | 2 | 3 |
| 4) He/she can understand my weaknesses. | 1 | 2 | 3 |
| 5) He/she tries to understand my point of view. | 1 | 2 | 3 |
| 6) He/she has an appreciation for my value as a human being. | 1 | 2 | 3 |
| 7) He/she cares enough to let me go, or even to give me up. | 1 | 2 | 3 |
| 8) One of his/her feelings for me might be described as a love for mankind. | 1 | 2 | 3 |
| 9) He/she demands my appreciation. | 3 | 2 | 1 |
| 10) Being rejected by him/her changes my feelings for him/her. | 3 | 2 | 1 |
| 11) His/her feeling for me has a quality of forgiveness. | 1 | 2 | 3 |
| 12) His/her feeling for me has a quality of patience. | 1 | 2 | 3 |
| 13) He/she can tell what I'm feeling even when I don't talk about it. | 1 | 2 | 3 |
| 14) His/her feeling for me has a quality of compassion or sympathy. | 1 | 2 | 3 |

15) He/she has a deep feeling of concern
for my welfare as a human being.     1     2     3

16) He/she feels I have great worth and
dignity.[1]                          1     2     3

*Scoring.* The scoring is to be done as it was in chapter 5. Add up your responses. The highest possible score is 48; the lowest score is 16.

Let's rate as follows:

40-48     Your spouse really does listen.
32-39     You feel your spouse doesn't always listen.
24-31     You feel your spouse seldom listens.
16-23     The active-listening skill needs a lot of work.

*Evaluation of the Questions.* After you have rated each other, go back to the rating statements and look at each response. These statements are adapted from Everett L. Shostrom's test called the "Caring Relationship Inventory." The statements are probing for empathy. Several statements are similar. I'll consider each separately, however.

1) "He/she understands the way I feel." The ideal answer is "yes." A truly empathic spouse will focus on the feelings and understand them. He will not dismiss them and tell you, "You shouldn't feel that way."

2) "He/she values me as an individual or unique person." The ideal answer is "yes." You should not be required to feel a particular way or feel as your spouse does in order to have value as an individual.

3) "He/she feels deeply my most painful feelings." The ideal answer is "yes." Your spouse is to do more than give mere mental assent to your hurt. He should feel it himself.

4) "He/she can understand my weaknesses." The ideal answer is "yes." We should be able to understand each other's weaknesses because we are in touch with our own. This is what put the Pharisees out of touch with the common man.

They just didn't see any weaknesses in themselves and were, therefore, intolerant of weakness in others.

Often husbands and wives are not understanding of each other for the same reasons. They see themselves as so spiritual they cannot understand why others are not as they are. They sound much like the Pharisee Jesus spoke of in the parable of the Pharisee and tax-gatherer. "The Pharisee stood and was praying thus to himself, 'God, I thank Thee that I am not like other people: swindlers, unjust, adulterers, or even like this tax-gatherer'" (Luke 18:11).

5) "He/she tries to understand my point of view." The ideal answer is "yes." We should be able to crawl inside each other's skin and look at life through each other's eyes. It does not mean that we have no opinion of our own. But it does mean that we can accurately perceive the other person's point of view.

6) "He/she has an appreciation for my value as a human being." The ideal answer is "yes." You should not be required to see things as your spouse does in order to be valued as a human being.

7) "He/she cares enough to let me go, or even to give me up." The ideal answer is "yes." Valuing a person's worth means a willingness to let go if that person feels that it is in his best interest. This is even true of a prodigal (Luke 15:11–32). When we respect another person's need to go his own way we create a climate for his return, should he discover that his way wasn't so good after all. Often what we cannot accomplish by preaching and moralizing we can accomplish by lovingly letting go. This is one of the cardinal rules in the treatment of alcoholics.

8) "One of his/her feelings for me might be described as a love for mankind." The ideal answer is "yes." Christians, above all, ought to be lovers of mankind, or, as Peter puts it, "Honor all men" (1 Peter 2:17). We are truly made in the image of God and are to be valued as such (Gen. 9:6).

9) "He/she demands my appreciation." The ideal an-

swer is "no." Appreciation is in order. But if you demand it, then it cannot be given willingly. You rob your spouse of a significant opportunity to show caring by demanding it. This is why possessiveness is so damaging to a relationship. You are robbed of the opportunity of *freely* loving. It is expected of you because your spouse owns you. This does not mean that you are free from your marital vows. It does mean that you are not clubbed over the head with demands.

10) "Being rejected by him/her changes my feelings for him/her." The ideal answer is "no." In every marriage we experience a certain degree of rebuff or lack of empathy. But it should not be so severe or chronic that it changes our feelings for our spouse.

11) "His/her feeling for me has a quality of forgiveness." The ideal answer is "yes." Forgiveness carries with it an understanding of how that person failed you. Even though Jesus Christ was sinless He still could understand how we can fail Him. The denial of Peter was met with a great deal of compassion (John 21:15–23).

12) "His/her feeling for me has a quality of patience." This is similar to the previous statement. Our patience with others shows our ability truly to put ourselves in that person's place. Often when we are impatient or unforgiving we place ourselves apart as being quite incapable of those failures. This is a Pharisaical attitude—and is the reason why the Pharisees were unforgiving. They lacked the human quality of empathy.

13) "He/she can tell what I'm feeling even when I don't talk about it." The ideal answer is "yes." If your spouse is tuned in to all of your non-verbal cues, he ought to be able to have some idea of what you're feeling.

14) "His/her feeling for me has a quality of compassion or sympathy." The ideal answer is "yes." Compassion and sympathy are closely related to empathy. It's another way of saying, "I care how you feel, and I feel it too."

15) "He/she has a deep feeling of concern for my welfare as a human being." The ideal answer is "yes." As with state-

ment 8 this statement focuses on that element of caring that
values man as a creature made in God's image.

16) "He/she feels I have great worth and dignity." The
ideal answer is "yes." As in statement 15 man has worth and
dignity as a person. For your spouse to make your worth and
dignity contingent upon your seeing things as he does denies
this.

*Summary.* Listening is intimately linked to the act of love
called "empathy." Carl R. Rogers, writing on the characteristics of a helping relationship, summarized the matter well
when he said this:

> Can I let myself enter fully into the world of his feelings
> and personal meanings, and see these as he does? Can I step
> into his private world so completely that I lose all desire to
> evaluate or judge it? Can I enter it so sensitively that I can
> move about in it freely, without trampling on meanings which
> are precious to him? Can I sense it so accurately that I can
> catch not only the meanings of his experience which are obvi-
> ous to him, but those meanings which are only implicit, which
> he sees only dimly or as confusion? Can I extend this under-
> standing without limit?
>
> . . . I am impressed with the fact that even a minimal
> amount of empathetic understanding—a bumbling and faulty
> attempt to catch the confused complexity of the client's
> meaning—is helpful, though there is no doubt that it is most
> helpful when I can see and formulate clearly the meanings of
> his experiencing which for him have been unclear and tangled.[2]

The "bumbling and faulty" empathy of husbands and
wives toward each other also is without a doubt helpful. You
need not be a pro to show empathy and listen.

8

# Honey, I Have a Problem

## —By André

THE SUMMER DAY DAWNED bright and sunny. A light breeze was blowing from the Pacific, but the water was calm—a perfect day for sailing.

Fay and I had agreed that I needed time out of doors by myself. Being alone on the ocean was a tonic for me. So I decided I'd trailer my little Coronodo 18 down to Seal Beach and spend the day on the water.

I didn't set a time to be home. I knew I wanted to be in by sunset, which would put me home about 9 P.M. But, as I later found out, Fay had other ideas.

The day was fabulous. The wind kicked up a little more than I had anticipated, so it was quite a challenge to keep myself from getting dumped in the water.

I was pooped when I got home. Bedtime would be early that night—I thought. I hadn't planned on a major confrontation with Fay!

As I ate a snack I noticed Fay giving me the freeze. I can always tell when she's unhappy with me. Her face is expressionless. She doesn't look at me and has nothing to say.

Finally I raked up the courage to ask what was wrong. Fay was angry. But she wanted me to know that the anger wasn't just over the events of that day. She felt angry every time I'd go sailing.

My usual pattern was to sail all day, come home late, and flop into bed exhausted, leaving no part of the day for companionship with her. Sailing was like everything else I did— all or nothing.

What had happened here? Though Fay wanted to be accepting of me, my behavior stood in the way of her having her own needs fulfilled—her need for companionship. By staying out all day and then going to bed exhausted when I came home, I was creating a situation that had become a problem to her.

## OWNING THE PROBLEM

In chapter 4 I said that "owning the problem" means that I approach the problem with the attitude that the problem exists because of the way *I* feel and not because the other person is bad or defective. I accept the responsibility for finding a problem in my relationship with my spouse.

Owning the problem is a non-codemning way of expressing your inability to accept your spouse's behavior. In the earlier chapters of this book, acceptance was stressed. But acceptance does not mean that you never have problems with your spouse's behavior. Indeed, certain behavior may ultimately bring about the ruin of the marriage. Adultery and alcoholism are just two of many such problems.

In stressing acceptance I have been attempting to show that we cannot solve our differences in marriage by convincing our spouse that he or she is a bad person in need of reform. God can do that. The Bible can do that. Preachers can do that. The court system and judges can do that. But in the everyday affairs of husbands and wives, the behaviors that need change are usually not critical enough and are too numerous to require authoritative outside intervention. And because a husband and wife are peers and equally the objects of God's grace, it is unwise for either to become the authoritative voice in the marriage (1 Peter 3:7; Gal. 3:28).

Instead of attempting to convince your spouse that he has a problem and is a bad person, perhaps the solution is to own the problem yourself.

"Owning the problem" is a non-condemning way of expressing your inability to accept your spouse's behavior. It is done by seeing it as your problem, not his.

Owning the problem is necessary when 1) your spouse's behavior blocks the fulfillment of your needs and 2) you cannot accept his behavior without modification.

*Avoid Condemnation.* When our spouse's behavior bothers us we tend to handle it by condemning it. And the better our knowledge of the Bible, the greater the temptation to bring the authority of Scripture to bear on that behavior. Now it may be true that the behavior is questionable in biblical terms. But are *you* the one to invoke the authority of Scripture? What is more, unless it is a clear case of sin, your interpretation will be challenged by the offending spouse. It may be challenged even in the case of sinful behavior. Husbands and wives resent it when the other becomes the authoritative guide in matters of morals or ethics. Indeed, I have seen right and righteous husbands and wives invoke the authority of Scripture only to lose an embittered spouse in divorce.

We easily fall into the trap of judging the behavior of other people. If they do what we want, they are good. If they don't, they are bad.

Recently I took my grandson Collin, age three, and granddaughter Stacy, age nine months, for a walk. I was pushing Stacy in her stroller and Collin was running ahead of us on the sidewalk pretending he was driving a car.

As we approached a cross-street I began to get anxious because I was afraid that he would run across the street ahead of me. So I called out, "Collin! Stop there and wait for papa."

He dutifully applied the brakes and stood there with his motor idling. When I caught up to him I said, "That's a good boy, Collin."

Then it hit me. Whether Collin's compliance with my wish was good or bad was beside the point. He simply was giving me what I needed to ease *my problem of anxiety*. As far as Collin was concerned, there was no problem! Grandpa had the problem. And when I recognized that it was *my* problem I responded differently.

At the next street the same thing happened, and I made the same request: "Please wait for me." But this time when he complied I said, "Thank you, Collin." And then said to myself, "Grandpa needed that."

It's true that Collin's safety was at stake and that was what made me anxious. But even then Collin was aware of no danger, and he might have waited for me at the cross-street without my asking. So really, the problem wasn't his; it was mine.

Now let's go back to my original description of "owning the problem." The situation with Collin fits. 1) His behavior was blocking the fulfillment of my need—the need to be free of anxiety. His running ahead of me blocked that need. 2) I could not accept his behavior without modification. He could run ahead, so long as it was not too far ahead, and he could do it if he waited for me to cross the street with him.

Collin's compliance in this case was not so much goodness or badness, smartness or dumbness. It had to do with *my* need. Because Collin loves and respects me he gave me what I needed.

*What to Do When You Own the Problem.* In order to deal with the problem in this example, I used the technique of "requesting."[1]

1) Requesting. When mutual respect and caring has been established between two people, a respectful request is

one way to deal with the problem. It is important that the request is framed in such a way as to make it sound like a respectful request. By that I mean that there should be no blaming, condemning, or judging. The tone of voice should convey respect.

Once again we are attempting to avoid setting up a judgmental situation. We are attempting to avoid the implication, "I have every right to expect this because I am right and you are wrong." Quite apart from right and wrong the message must be, "I need this for me. Will you give it to me?"

2) Suggesting alternatives. Perhaps your spouse's behavior might be more acceptable to you under different conditions. Earlier I used the illustration of sailing. Fay was not against my sailing. She could handle my being away from her doing my thing so long as I reserved time and energy for her. So she suggested I come home a little earlier. And this alternative has worked well.

3) Direct sending. When all else fails, direct sending is useful. Direct sending is a direct expression of your *feelings* about the unacceptable behavior. Note that I emphasize *feelings*. Moralizing and judging the behavior will lead to conflict. But the expression of your feelings in a non-judgmental way is much less threatening, and you are more likely to be heard. When you do this you don't judge your spouse. But you do let him know that you can't help having negative feelings about his behavior.

The direct sending of feelings is done in the form of "I" messages. An "I" message is a *report* of the impact of the spouse's behavior on you. I emphasize *report* because we must distinguish between judging the behavior and sharing our feelings about the behavior. Or, to put it another way, it's reporting the problem in terms of where *you* are and not in terms of your spouse's badness. Often I preface "I" messages with, "Honey, I have a problem."

*"I" Messages.* Here's how to do it.

| BEHAVIOR ("When") | EMOTION ("I feel") | IMPACT ("Because") |
|---|---|---|

1) Husband comes home late with no prior explanation. Wife says:

| "When I don't know where you are . . ." | "I feel anxious . . ." | "because I'm afraid something has happened to you." |
|---|---|---|

2) Wife does not keep house neat. The husband says:

| "When the house looks cluttered . ." | "I feel annoyed . . ." | "because I think I'm working harder at my job than you are at yours." |
|---|---|---|

In neither case is the spouse accused of being a bad person. In both cases the problem is expressed as though the problem is his own. The second example may open the sensitive subject of role expectations. But it does it in a non-attacking way.

*Why "I" Messages?* The *ICT Manual* has some good things to say about parent/child communication that can be adapted to husband/wife communication.[2] "I" messages are important because:

1) They show ownership of the problem.

2) They communicate honesty and openness.

3) They communicate to the spouse the effect of the behavior, which is far less threatening than the suggestion that something is bad about him because he has engaged in certain behavior.

4) They place a responsibility on the spouse for modifying his behavior and provide opportunities to be considerate of the needs and feelings of others.

5) They demonstrate respect for the spouse and at the same time show that your needs are important too.

6) They provide a means for being honest. When you share your feelings, your spouse will be more willing to do so when he has a problem.

7) They tell your spouse how you *feel,* which is less threatening than accusing him of causing those feelings.

8) They deal with actions or behavior, not his self-esteem. They do not attack personality or character. We have a right to question a spouse's behavior. But we have no right to question him as a person or his worth as a creature made in God's image.

9) They communicate trust—trust that the spouse will respond to negative feelings which change when his behavior is blocking the fulfillment of the other spouse's needs.

10) They encourage the spouse to help with and share in the problem.

11) They provide a way for the spouse to know the limits of your acceptance.

12) They demonstrate that personal worth is not dependent on performance. Personal worth is not subject to cancellation with every misstep. A person with high self-esteem knows that his behavior does not always please, but knows that his spouse loves him. We can modify our behavior. But it's difficult to correct feelings of low self-esteem.

13) They build high self-esteem by reinforcing positive behavior. Direct "I" messages should express acceptable behaviors as well. For example, "When I hear you set aside the requests of others in favor of my requests, I feel loved, because it makes me feel as if you're willing to put me first."

## COMMUNICATION BREAKDOWN

We don't always send our messages effectively. Instead of "I" messages we often send "you" messages. A "you" message results in communication breakdown because the use of "you" implies that the other person is wrong and the speaker is right. These include blaming, name-calling, sarcasm, and analyzing, to name a few.

*"You" Messages and Sending Errors.* A "you" message is any message that conveys the idea that I am the normal one, I am right, and you are abnormal, defective, or wrong. Consider the following:

| SITUATION AND MESSAGE | SENDING ERROR |
|---|---|
| 1) Marlene, an atractive young woman is *very* attentive to your husband at a social event, and he is very responsive to her. You are hurt and angry. When you get home you say, "You certainly made a fool of yourself tonight. You acted as if your brain was addled with Marlene's attention." | Name calling ("You fool) Sarcasm ("Your brain was addled") |
| 2) Your wife has criticized your teen-age son for poor personal hygiene and a messy room. You are unhappy with the way she has handled it, and you say, "You shouldn't talk to Jeff like that. Don't you know that a lot of his behavior is your fault?" | Criticism, analyzing, fault-finding |

In these examples the messages clearly are, "There is something wrong with you." How might you correct these sending errors? Give it a try. 1) Tune in to your *feelings* toward the situation. 2) *Express* your feelings in terms of where *you are.* Own the problem as your own. Send an "I" message rather than a "you" message.

Did you try it? How did you do? Here are some examples of how the messages might have been handled differently:

"When it seemed as if Marlene was exceptionally attentive tonight and as if she was getting a lot of response, [A] I really felt angry and insecure [B] because another woman was getting what I wanted. [C]

Let's examine that message by the phrases marked A, B, and C.

A) "It seemed . . ." The wife is not accusing Marlene or her husband of anything. She is only reporting her view of the situation.

B) "I really felt angry and insecure . . ." She is being honest about feelings generated by what she thought she was seeing. Right or wrong, she was having those feelings, and they were affecting her relationship with her husband.

C) "Because another woman . . ." The report includes the impact of what she was seeing and the reason for her feelings. Another woman is taking her place (at least this is her view of the matter).

The response shows several things. The wife owns the problem. She expresses it in terms of her perception. She reports her feelings without defense of herself. She gives the reason for her feelings without attack on her husband.

Let's consider the second example, that of the husband who criticizes and blames his wife.

"When I heard the conversation with Jeff[A] I was irritated[B] because of the way it was handled."[C]

A) "When I heard . . ." He is not attacking his wife when he talks about his son and the problem.

B) "I was irritated . . ." He is reporting his negative reaction to what he heard without accusing his wife of being a bad person.

C) "Over the way it was handled." Again, he does not attack his wife for the way it was handled. He is only saying that it made him irritated.

*Poorly Coded Messages and Communication Breakdown.* Sometimes communication breakdown occurs because of a poorly coded message. A poorly coded message is one that lacks sufficient information for understanding. Or, to put it another way, the meaning cannot be understood or decoded because something has been left out. Poorly coded messages usually leave out what the speaker is thinking, feeling, or intending. And when the listener does not act on the message, the speaker is hurt or disappointed.

Fay and I had a problem with a poorly coded message over the sale of our vacation home (which we finally decided not to sell). I had put up a "for sale" sign, and our neighbor, Bill, offered to show the house when we weren't there. As winter approached Fay suggested that we take down the sign.

When I asked why, she said that most interested buyers come by in the summertime and not during the winter.

I replied that there was enough winter traffic to warrant leaving the sign up. At that, Fay became visibly annoyed at me and said, "Forget about it."

I was hurt and angry. What had I done to deserve such a response? So I pursued the matter further.

Her response was, "I'm just trying to think of other people's feelings." The implication was: Andy isn't sensitive to the feelings of other people.

That hurt and baffled me even more. Then it came out what she was *thinking, feeling,* and *intending.*

The day before, Bill said that fifteen people had come by to see the house the previous weekend. He put it in such a way that Fay thought he was annoyed at having to show the house. I took it to mean, "I'm being a good neighbor by showing your house for you."

Fay didn't tell me that she *thought* Bill was annoyed and that she *felt* we were imposing on him. Her *intention* was to correct this imposition.

When she spoke to me about the sign, she didn't tell me her thoughts, feelings, or intentions. All she gave me was the message: "Let's take down the sign for the winter." What is more, she complicated the message by telling me she thought the winter traffic wouldn't justify leaving it up.

Not knowing her real thoughts, feelings, and intentions, I reacted only to the message. And it was a reaction that she didn't like because it blocked the fulfillment of her need—the need not to impose on Bill. When I did understand, we were able to talk about it more constructively.

Did you notice that there was another poorly coded message in that incident? It was Bill's message. He told us that fifteen people had come by to see the house the weekend before. But he told us nothing else. What were *his* thoughts, feelings, and intentions?

I thought he was saying, "I'm a good neighbor [his

thought], and I want you to feel good about me [his intention] by knowing that I'm pleased to show your house to so many people [his feeling]."

Fay thought he was saying, "There are limits to my being a good neighbor [his thought], and I want you to know that showing your house is a burden [his intention], and I really don't feel like doing it any more [his feeling]."

After realizing that Bill had given us a poorly coded message we decided that we ought to find out what he really meant before acting on it. But then we didn't have to because we decided not to sell! It was worth it all as an exercise in communication.

*The Minnesota Couples' Communication Program* handbook says that we can avoid this kind of breakdown through a process called "shared meaning."

> Shared meaning is a process of making sure that the "message sent" is the same as the "message received." It's a process of "tuning-in" to each other, of trying to help each other understand what you think, feel, and intend, *and* realize that understanding has occurred. *Both* the sender and the receiver are involved, and both have responsibilities.
>
> For the sender, the prime responsibility is clarity of expression. He must be certain of what he wants to say, and express it clearly and completely.
>
> The receiver's prime responsibility is to observe and listen attentively, and to report back *all* the messages he receives (both verbal and non-verbal messages). In the act of reporting back, the receiver is acknowledging that he has received a message and indicates what messages he has received.
>
> At this point, the sender has a very important responsibility—to *acknowledge that he* received his partner's report by either confirming the accuracy of the report . . . or by giving more information to clarify his original message. Of course, a shared meaning is achieved only when the sender acknowledges the accuracy of the receiver's report.
>
> Notice! Final responsibility for determining whether the message sent is the same as the message received lies with the

*sender* because only the sender knows what the original message is.[3]

*Summary.* Sending effective messages requires that we are careful not to make the listener feel attacked. By giving "I" messages rather than "you" messages we enable the listener to hear what we're saying.

Respect and acceptance of the other person does not mean that you have no self-respect or convictions of your own or that anything goes. You are to have self-respect too. In fact, if both the husband and wife do not have a high degree of self-respect and limits to what they will accept, the relationship will be sick.

Self-respect and limits to what you will accept must be conveyed to your spouse. But how you do it is all important. It is important also that you not defend or justify your own position. People *who care about each other* need not defend or justify themselves.

9

# Shifting Gears: The Art of Talking and Listening

## —BY ANDRÉ

MUCH COMMUNICATION IN MARRIAGE is a simple exchange of information. For example:

*He:* "What time is the meeting tonight?"

*She:* "Eight o'clock."

### SHIFTING GEARS

There's no problem with that kind of exchange. We have seen, however, that conversing about a problem requires a little more of us. Effective communication involves a sender who sends "I" messages and a listener who actively listens. Consider the following example:

*She* ("I" message): When I saw you and Marlene talking last night, I felt angry because I thought she was getting more attention than I.

*He* (active-listening and avoiding defense): It sounds as if you felt left out and neglected by me.

*She* ("I" message): Yes, but there's more. I felt angry at both of you because it seemed that she was giving a come on, and you were enjoying it.

*He* (active-listening and not taking issue with her interpretation of the behavior): It looked to you as if some not-so-innocent flirting was going on.

*She:* Exactly!

Even though the husband has not interrupted and has made his wife feel that she has been heard, he may have a view of the problem that is different from hers. How does he get to express *his point of view?* After all, different people have different feelings about the same situation. The answer is that he and his wife "shift gears."

*What Is "Shifting Gears?"* Shifting gears is simply the process of change from sending to receiving. He now shifts from active-listening to sending "I" messages, and she shifts from sending "I" messages to active-listening. The sequence might go as follows:

*He:* This opens a subject that I've been wanting to talk about. (He then sends an "I" message): When we're out in public together, I feel inhibited, because I think you may be jealous of the time I spend with others—both men and women.

*She* (active-listening): It sounds as if you're saying that I tend to throw a wet blanket on social activity when we're out.

*He* ("I" message): Yes. I understand your concern over my behavior with women, but I feel inhibited in getting acquainted with others because I think I should stay by your side for the whole evening.

*She* (active-listening): So you're saying that the issue is larger than just Marlene.

*He:* Yes. Exactly!

At this point we don't have a solution, but by shifting gears—each taking turns at sending and receiving—they both are getting a clearer picture of the problem. It's likely that the husband's input will stir further feelings in the wife that she needs to get out, so they'll shift gears again. She will become the sender and he the receiver.

*She* ("I" message): It's true that I find myself getting tense when we're out socially, and I think it's because I feel insecure with you.

*He* (active-listening): I hear you saying that I'm doing something to make you feel insecure.

*She* ("I" message): I feel hurt often because it seems I need you more than you need me.

*He* (active-listening): Could you help me understand that a little better?

*She* ("I" message): It seems that you are content with your own life and your own friends, and I have a very small part in your life so I feel left out, hurt, and angry.

This conversation should be permitted to develop until she has gotten out all her feelings. It may be that the husband will have more feelings to share when she is done, so that means that they should shift gears again. He again becomes the sender and she the receiver.

Shifting gears enables each to clearly and completely state feelings and the reason for them *without interruption*. It provides an orderly process for the sharing of new feelings as the problem unfolds.

Talking out the problem in this manner may not yield an immediate solution. But the husband and wife will know exactly how the other one thinks and feels. This will enable them to propose solutions that both can live with. Many times couples can't solve their problems because *they don't know what the problem is.* They have not tried to *understand* each other. Each is more interested in building his own case and destroying the other's.

Shifting gears is, then, an orderly process whereby two people can share their feelings without fear of interruption and can do it with the assurance that they will be heard. It is done by taking turns at sending "I" messages and receiving as an active-listener.

The three sequences on this page and the previous pages might be diagrammed as follows:

> She sends the "I" message.
> He receives by active-listening.
>> *shift gears*
> He sends the "I message.
> She receives by active-listening.
>> *shift gears*
> She sends the "I" message.
> He receives by active-listening.

*Problems To Watch When Shifting Gears.* Be sure you watch out for these typical problems when you're trying to shift gears.

1) Be careful not to send "you" messages. When feelings are hot you might resort to attacking. Remember that "you" messages are the language of attack. Good communication demands an "I" message that reports where the speaker is, not a "you" message that tells the listener how bad he is.

2) Defensiveness. It's never pleasant to hear that you have made someone else unhappy. You will be tempted to defend yourself by denying the validity of what is being said or by counterattacking.

3) Fear of Anger. Real feelings need to come out so you can deal with the real problems. Often the presenting problem is only the "tip of the iceberg." The "presenting problem" is the problem that is presented or offered as the cause of the trouble. Sometimes it is the cause of the trouble, but the problem usually goes much deeper, as was demonstrated previously in the dialogue on Marlene. Shifting gears is an unfolding process that enables a couple to thoroughly explore the presenting and related problems without damaging each other's worth, but this does not preclude the expression of anger.

4) Telling the other person how he feels. Sometimes when an "I" message is sent, the listener does not listen, but tells the speaker that he does not feel that way. For example, suppose I tell you that I'm hurt because you treated me badly. Instead of listening to my feelings you say, "You don't feel

hurt. You're really mad because you didn't get your way." Don't do that. Listen to how I say I feel. Don't correct me and tell me how I "really" feel.

5) Rushing the process. When feelings are hot the temptation is to unload all at once. Unload slowly and pause between active-listening and sending your own "I" message. If you rush in with your own "I" message, the other person will not feel that you have listened.

## INVENTORY OF COMMUNICATION SKILLS

Now let's take inventory of our talking and listening skills. Some of these I have already mentioned. Others I want to add at this point.

*Speaking for Yourself.* The "I" message is a way of speaking for yourself. It should involve a total expression of your own thoughts, feelings, intentions, and sensations. You are an authority on yourself, and no one else can know what's going on inside you unless you tell him.

Speaking for yourself also means not speaking for others. Sometimes we try to reinforce our case by saying things like, "I'm not the only one who feels that way. Your children [or parents or friends] all say the same thing." That's bound to invite defense. You can speak with authority on your own thoughts, feelings, intentions, and sensations, but you invite trouble when you speak for others.

For example, a wife may say, "I'm really hurt and angry because it seems you spend more time on the golf course than with me." But the husband replies, "That's not how you feel. You just don't like my golfing buddy George." Who is he to speak with such authority about what his wife *really* thinks and feels?

Sometimes there is an *incongruence* in what people say, which leads to confusion and doubt about what they really intend to say. Incongruence means that what they say (words) and how they say it (behavior) don't seem to match.

Sometimes the problem is a *double message*. One thing is said today and a different thing is said tomorrow. But these problems are not dealt with by correcting the other person. They are corrected with an "I" message.

Let's go back to the problem of incongruence. The husband might deal with the problem by saying, "Honey, I'm confused. When I hear you're angry that I don't spend more time with you, I don't know what to think. It seems to me that the problem is your dislike of George, not my neglecting you." The husband would then describe the incongruence to her. For example, if the husband golfs by himself, the wife hardly complains at all. If he golfs with George, she complains. She says that the problem is the time her husband spends away from her, golfing. When George goes along, her husband spends the same amount of time away, but she goes into orbit. The question of incongruence is this: how come, if her problem is her husband's being away, she complains when George goes, but doesn't complain when her husband goes alone? She *says* the problem is time, but *acts* as if the problem is George.

*Describing Behavior.* People communicate verbally and non-verbally. Many times another person's behavior will be misinterpreted.

One day Fay and I were at Disneyland, and we ran into some people whom I had met at a conference. Fay didn't know them. As they greeted me I noticed that Fay was silent and moved from my side to a position slightly behind me. It seemed to me that she was hiding behind me and didn't want to be introduced. I also thought that she might resent these friends taking away from our time together. So I made the conversation as short as I could politely, and we moved on.

I noticed she was quiet but didn't think much about it until we got home and I saw that she was still quiet and withdrawn. Something was wrong.

When I asked her about it, she said that she felt hurt. I hadn't introduced her to my friends at Disneyland.

When I described her behavior and how I interpreted it, she was surprised. She said that she did feel a bit awkward since I knew the people and she didn't. But she did expect an introduction.

What was the problem? I was misinterpreting the behavior I was seeing. Many times communication breakdown occurs because we incorrectly interpret another person's behavior. This can be corrected by describing the behavior and how we interpret it.

For example: "When I see you smile like that, I think that you're happy, and I want to hug you." Or, "When I see that far-away look it seems as if you're not there, and I feel lonely." Or, "When you seem cold and distant, I wonder if something's wrong with our relationship."

*Making Feeling Statements.* In chapter 8 we saw that the "I" message is a statement of our *feelings* and the reason for those feelings. An "I" message is not an opinion. The listener may argue with your opinions and consider his own opinion just as good. He will resist your moralizing, blaming, judging, and condemning. But when you say how you feel without attacking him for creating those feelings, you are most likely to be heard.

Sometimes an unhelpful listener will say, "You shouldn't feel that way because after all . . ." and then proceed to give reasons why. When that happens, you have another problem. You might just say it: "When I hear that I shouldn't feel that way, I feel hurt, angry, and not understood."

*Making Intention Statements.* In the illustration of selling our vacation home I pointed out that a properly coded message requires a statement of intention. Was it Bill's intention to let us know that he was being a good neighbor, or was it his intention to tell us that showing the house was a big nuisance? His intention was all-important to our understanding the rest of his message and how we should react to it.

*Asking the Other To Reflect Back Your Message.* Active-listening should give the speaker the feeling that he's really being heard and understood. If you're not sure that you've been listened to, you can ask the other person what he heard you say. This is called "shared meaning." [1] Your spouse knows what you mean, and he knows that you feel understood.

*Acknowledging the Other Person's Message.* You need not wait for the other person to ask if you understood. You may take the initiative by acknowledging it.

Saying, "I heard you," is not acknowledging. We acknowledge when we give sufficient feedback, such as, "I hear you saying that you get mad at me when you're trying to talk to me, and I have my eyes glued to the TV set. The TV seems more important than you."

*Checking Out.* Sometimes sending and listening start with "checking out." This is a way of finding out where the other person is in his thoughts, feelings, and intentions. When a husband and wife have been away from each other for awhile, they unconsciously check out each other when they meet again.

First, they look for non-verbal clues. Does the expression on the face, the tone of the voice, and the body language indicate that all is well? Or do you detect uneasiness, aloofness, coolness, anger, distress, or a negative feeling of any kind?

Second, you look for verbal clues. What is the person saying? Is the context of what he's saying cheerful and upbeat, or is it negative? When he says these things, what is he thinking and feeling? What are his intentions, based on what he is saying?

Third, you look for incongruence. Does what he is saying and how he is saying it go together? Does he use cheerful words, but reveal non-verbal distress. In such a case, describing behavior would be a helpful way to "check out."

## WHEN COMMUNICATION BREAKDOWN OCCURS

It's inevitable that couples will experience communication breakdown no matter how pure their intentions. Our sin nature tends to get in the way. And the usual culprits are attack and defense. We seem to have a desperate need to prove ourselves right and the other person wrong.

*Metacommunicate.* What do we do when that happens? The answer is to "metacommunicate." The prefix "meta" means here "to go beyond" what you are talking about and examine *how you're doing it* and *what is happening.* The moment you discover that communication is breaking down, *stop,* and ask yourselves what's going wrong.

*Example of Metacommunication.* Let's go back to the incident with Marlene and see how communication breakdown might occur and how either the husband or wife might metacommunicate instead.

*She* ("I" message): When I saw you and Marlene talking last night I felt angry because I thought she was getting more attention than I.

*(no active-listening)*

*He* (defensively): What do you mean by that? I was not giving her more attention than you!

*(new "I" message because of breakdown)*

*She* (metacommunicating): Honey, I'm having another problem right now. When I get a response like that, I feel frustrated, because I don't think I've been heard and understood.

Now the husband well-versed in communication will stop defending himself right there. The incorrigible will ignore the wife's attempt to metacommunicate and continue with his defense.

In such a case it would be wise for the wife not to return to the discussion about Marlene. She has a more basic problem. She and her husband don't communicate. She might more profitably address their communication problems. They may need professional help if they can't talk about their inability to talk.

*Roadblock Check List.* In the above example the communication breakdown occurred because of the husband's defensiveness. Here's a check list of other roadblocks to good communication.

1) Directing, ordering, commanding, such as, "You must have my breakfast ready by six A.M." ("You have to . . ." "You will . . .")

2) Warning, threatening, admonishing, such as, "You had better get yourself home directly after work." ("If you don't, then . . .")

3) Moralizing, preaching, obliging, such as, "You should tithe regularly." ("You ought . . ." "It is your duty . . ." "It is your responsibility . . ." "You are required . . .")

4) Persuading with logic, arguing, instructing, lecturing, such as, "Do you realize that well-bred people simply don't do that?" ("Here is why you are wrong . . ." "That is not right . . ." "Yes, but . . .")

5) Advising, recommending, providing answers or solutions, such as, "What I would do is tell the boss that he was unfair." ("Why don't you . . ." "Let me suggest . . ." "It would be best for you . . .")

6) Evaluating, judging negatively, disapproving, blaming, name-calling, criticizing, such as, "You are bad!" ("You are lazy." "You are not thinking straight." "You are acting foolishly.")

7) Praising, judging or evaluating positively, approving, such as, "You're a good husband." ("You've done a good job." "I approve of . . ." "That's a nice thing to do.")

8) Supporting, reassuring, excusing, sympathizing, such as, "It's not so bad; things will look different tomorrow." ("Don't worry." "You'll feel better." "That's too bad.")

9) Diagnosing, psychoanalyzing, reading-in, offering in-

sights, interpreting, such as, "What you need is to get your life straight with God!" ("What's wrong with you is . . ." "You're just trying to get attention." "You don't really mean that." "I know what you need." "Your problem is . . .")

10) Questioning, probing, cross-examining, prying, interrogating, such as, "Why do you always spend so much time on the phone with George?" ("Who . . ." "Where . . ." "What . . ." "How . . ." "When . . .")

11) Diverting, avoiding, by passing, disagreeing, shifting, silence, such as, "Let's not talk about it now." ("Not at the dinner table." "Forget it." "That reminds me." "We can discuss it later.")

12) Kidding, teasing, making light of, joking, using sarcasm, such as, "Why don't you shoot the boss?" ("When did you read a newspaper last?" "Get up on the wrong side of the bed, did you?" "When did they make you President of the Corporation?")

13) Comparing, such as, "Why can't you be like Martha's husband?" ("When I was a kid . . .")

10

# Awareness: What's Going On Inside You and Me?

## —BY FAY

ANOTHER LIGHT TURNED ON in my quest for self-aware-ness and good communication with Andy. We had been shop-ping with our son and his friend, and decided to eat our eve-ning meal at a nearby restaurant. When we got there we found a line and were told to expect a wait of fifteen minutes to a half an hour.

We got in line and waited awhile, but I thought I was picking up from Andy impatience at having to wait. To please him (so I thought) I offered to fix a meal at home so he wouldn't have to wait. I didn't tell him that I would rather have waited in line than cook a meal and wash dishes. This didn't come out until afterwards.

Later in our conversation about the evening, the subject of the line came up. Imagine my surprise when I discovered that Andy would have been willing to wait in line if he had known that I really didn't want to come home and fix a meal! Both of us learned a lot from this experience: the importance of total awareness. My needs went begging because I interpreted what I thought Andy was feeling without adequate awareness of what really was going on inside him. He was ready to wait in line as long as it took if I really wanted to eat there. And even though I did want to eat there I gave him a false signal about my feelings and told him that I didn't care!

All the principles in chapters 1 through 9 cannot be applied without awareness. We must be in touch with what's going on inside ourselves and each other. Effective talking and listening depend on it.

The *Minnesota Couples' Communication Program* handbook has an excellent chapter on awareness that zeros in on five sources of information we need to be aware of. They are your *senses*, your *interpretations*, your *feelings*, your *intentions*, and your *expressions* (how you express yourself). Let's look at each of these and see the important place they play in good communication.

## Your Senses

We have five senses: touch, smell, sight, taste, and sound. Whenever husbands and wives are together, their senses pick up information about each other.

"I hear your voice growing louder."

"I feel stiffness and distance when I hug you."

"I see a frown on your face."

All of these are undeniable signals our senses pick up. But be careful that you are not quick to interpret what you sense. A lot of times communication goes awry because we interpret what we sense without adequate information. If we hear the voice growing louder, feel stiffness, and see a frown we may interpret that as rejection before we have enough information to do so.

Let's say in this case that a wife is sensing these things in her husband and interprets them as rejection. But the husband is just tired and irritable from a bad day at work and impossible commuter traffic. He has no intention of rejecting his wife. He just wants to be left alone long enough to catch his breath. If his wife is hostile toward him because she interprets rejection, he will feel that her hostility is unjustified. He will probably react with hostility himself. Once the chain reaction starts, it's only a matter of time before there's a big explosion, with accusations flying in all directions.

When you sense something in your spouse that concerns or bothers you, *check it out* before you interpret what you assume he's thinking, feeling, or intending. This is done by describing what you are sensing. Technically it's called "documenting behavior." And you describe it in an "I" message.

"Honey, when I hear your voice get louder and see a frown on your face, it makes me feel uneasy because I think I have done something to displease you." He then has a responsibility to tell you what's going on inside him. His day has been difficult, and he just needs time to recover.

When Andy and I were waiting in line at the restaurant, I failed to do this. I should have checked out what I thought was his impatience with the long line. Of course, he also needed to know that I really wanted to eat there and did *not* want to go home and cook and wash dishes. But I acted as if it didn't matter, and when he sensed that, he misinterpreted me and suggested we go home. Both of us were guilty of misinterpreting what we were sensing in the other.

## YOUR INTERPRETATIONS

Let me repeat the caution stated earlier. Be sure your interpretation is correct by checking it out.

Be aware, however, that sometimes we run into problems in checking out. The husband who had a bad day may have difficulty answering if he really doesn't know what's bothering him. Limited awareness frequently causes communication problems. Husbands and wives owe it to each other to get in touch with what's going on inside of themselves so they can share that information with each other. Yes, this makes us vulnerable to each other. But there's no intimacy without vulnerability.

Sometimes your attempts to check out the meaning of certain behavior will be met with: "Wrong? Why, nothing's wrong." But you know there is. He says nothing's wrong, but he's stiff, distant, and is frowning. This is an "incongruent message." His words and actions don't go together.

When that happens, you have a second problem. Not only is something wrong, he's unwilling to talk about what's bothering him. Further attempts to document his behavior may make him angry. As we will point out in this book, not everyone who says he wants to communicate really wants to. The fear of vulnerability is often too great.

## YOUR FEELINGS

Being out of touch with our feelings is a common reason for poor communication. And the problem seems to be greater among Christians who are judgmental about certain negative feelings such as hurt, anger, and depression. They don't think they should have those feelings, so they block out awareness of them and look for other circumstances on which to hang their feelings.

As a result, they never get around to talking about the real issue—how they feel about neglect, rejection, or abandonment. They may talk about what *ought* to be done on their behalf, footnoted with appropriate Scripture. But they are not comfortable with talking about their feelings.

*Denial of Feelings.* I think this is due in part to a denial of their humanity—at least the feeling dimension of it. The intellect and will are very prominent, but the feelings are ignored. The formula seems to be: We are to know what God wants (exercise of the intellect) and are to do it (exercise of the will), but ignore how we feel about it (denial of the feelings).

Certainly we should not let our feelings run rampant and control our lives. But awareness of how we feel is an important function of our humanity and is essential to communication. Often marriage problems are not due to people being poor

Christians. Some problems are due to their not being good human beings—they are unaware of their feelings.

Jesus in His earthly ministry first gave attention to the feelings of people—their hurts—before He sermonized and told them what to do. This is what distinguished His ministry from that of the scribes and Pharisees, who didn't seem to care that people were hurting. Promising relief from the religious burdens of the day, Jesus said that His yoke was easy and His burden light (Matt. 11:28 30). This stood in contrast to the terrible load the Pharisees put on the people, a load that they were unwilling to help the people bear (Matt. 23:1–4). Feeling Jesus' concern over their hurts, the people were ready to hear what He had to say about the problem of sin.

*Looking for Scapegoats.* Even when we try to understand why we feel as we do, we still may come up with the wrong reason because we're afraid to face the truth. I sometimes silently blame Andy for making me feel guilty for not dieting and exercising because he's so dedicated to diet and physical fitness. I feel irritated when I see him eat boiled chicken, and I'm eating an ice cream sundae!

No matter how many times he tells me that he's dieting and working out for himself and that it's up to me what I do for myself, I still feel irritated. If he wouldn't diet and exercise, *I* wouldn't feel guilty! But I know that's unfair to him. This is really something I put on myself.

Because I tend to have feelings of low self-worth I easily interpret the words and behavior of other people as a negative commentary on me. And I find that these feelings also are at the root of cutting and unkind things I say.

*Opinions and Feelings.* Another impediment to awareness of feelings is that many people confuse opinions and feelings. Instead of stating a feeling, they state an opinion. Opinions are intellectual and safe. Feelings can wipe you out.

You can be sure an opinion is being expressed if you use

the word "that" in your statement. Say for example a husband feels put down and humiliated by his wife because she always disparages what he says. How is he going to deal with that? He may say, "I don't think you ought to talk to me like that!" But that's an opinion she might argue with. She might say, "Why not? You're always saying stupid things." On the other hand he may say, "When my ideas are disparaged, I feel put down and humiliated." This is not an opinion but a feeling. He is not talking about whose opinion is correct—a nice intellectual exercise. He is talking about feelings that hurt. He feels put down and humiliated.

Many couples never get down to serious communication because they argue over whose opinion is correct rather than care about each other's feelings. And whether or not I think you should feel as you do, caring about your feelings can go a long way to good communication.

Remember that "I" messages depend on your being aware of your feelings. Whenever you have a difficult time putting together an "I" message, get in touch with how you feel first. When you are aware of the feeling, then you can put together the "I" message.

Take the case of the husband with the disparaging wife mentioned earlier. His feeling was that of humiliation and put-down. So a complete "I" message would be, "When I try to say something intelligent to you [behavior] I feel humiliated [emotion] because what I say is always disparaged [impact]."

When you don't know how you feel, it may help to take a look at this word list of feelings. Look it over, decide how you're feeling and why you're feeling that way. Then try to put it into an "I" message.

| HATE | FEAR | ANGER | HAPPINESS |
|------|------|-------|-----------|
| 1. dislike | 1. fright | 1. sore | 1. joyful |
| 2. bitter | 2. terror | 2. offended | 2. enthusiastic |
| 3. hateful | 3. anxious | 3. mad | 3. merry |
| 4. odious | 4. misgivings | 4. resentful | 4. lucky |

| | | | |
|---|---|---|---|
| 5. detest | 5. concern | 5. wrathful | 5. fortunate |
| 6. spiteful | 6. harassed | 6. hostile | 6. pleased |
| 7. aversion | 7. dread | 7. displeased | 7. glad |
| 8. despise | 8. alarm | 8. injured | 8. satisfied |
| 9. loathe | 9. apprehension | 9. vexed | 9. contented |
| 10. abominable | 10. worry | 10. torment | 10. delighted |

| LOVE | DISAPPOINTMENT | SADNESS | CONFUSION |
|---|---|---|---|
| 1. affection | 1. disturbed | 1. tearful | 1. mixed-up |
| 2. loving | 2. unhappy | 2. grief | 2. doubtful |
| 3. amorous | 3. unsatisfied | 3. dejected | 3. disorder |
| 4. likable | 4. frustrated | 4. torment | 4. bewilderment |
| 5. tenderness | 5. deluded | 5. anguish | 5. confounded |
| 6. devotion | 6. defeated | 6. sorrow | 6. disarray |
| 7. attachment | 7. hurt | 7. unhappy | 7. jumble |
| 8. fondness | 8. failure | 8. gloomy | 8. uncertain |
| 9. passion | 9. rejection | 9. melancholy | 9. perplexed |
| 10. endearing | 10. thwarted | 10. mournful | 10. embarrassment[1] |

## YOUR INTENTIONS

Let's say that your senses have gathered information, you have properly interpreted it, and you have feelings about it. What do you intend to do about it? Nothing? Well, that's still a decision.

Failure to understand what is intended in communication frequently leads to communication breakdown and misunderstanding. Consider this example:

Andy has been jogging and brings home a lot of sweaty, dirty clothes. He *feels* guilty for adding to my already large laundry. With the intention of relieving his guilt and being helpful, he loads up the washer and says to me (for my approval), "I put a load of clothes in the washer." Now maybe I've been feeling guilty for letting the laundry slip. Since I don't know what his *intention* was, I feel angry because he's acting as though I can't keep up with the laundry, and he has to help. My *intention* is to get back at him. So I look in the washer and say disgustedly, "When are you going to learn to sort out clothes and not wash everything together?"

The situation is now ripe for disaster. Here the poor man has tried to be helpful, and I cut him down!

Disaster is averted by talking about our feelings and intentions. I discover that his feeling is guilt and his intention is to be helpful, not critical. He discovers that my feeling is anger and that my intention was to defend myself against attack.

*I'm Angry Because You're Angry.* Often when an intention is misunderstood it leads to a peculiar kind of discord that I call, "I'm angry because you're angry." When I didn't understand Andy's intention, suppose I had said to him angrily, "I wish you'd leave my washing machine alone and quit messing up my laundry." He most likely would have gotten angry and said, "Well, forget about my being helpful the next time."

*Fay:* "What are you getting angry about? You were the one who messed up the laundry."

*Andy:* "I'm angry because you're angry. You have no right to be angry at me when I was just trying to be helpful!"

Andy would not be justified in his anger. If he made his intention clear, there would have been no misunderstanding. The sender has a responsibility to give a clear message. If his intentions are good, yet unclear, he must not find fault with the receiver for not seeing his good intentions.

*Unaware Intentions.* Let me offer another example. Let's say that a husband and wife are at a party and the husband, in his wife's opinion, seems too attentive to an attractive young woman. If the wife is not totally aware of her interpretations, feelings, intentions, and expressions, poor communication will be the result.

Sense—Husband is attentive to sweet-young-thing.
Interpretation—"He'd rather be with her than me."
Feeling—Anger.
Intention—Unaware.
Expression—"You sure looked sloppy tonight."

Because the wife was unaware of the intention behind her expression, her husband will probably miss the purpose of the sarcasm and only be irritated. If his wife were in touch with what she wanted to do (her intentions), she would realize that she wanted to punish him by making him feel he looked like a slob to the sweet-young-thing.

When there is total self-awareness the sequence should go like this:

Sense—Husband is attentive to sweet-young-thing.
Interpretation—"He'd rather be with her than me."
Feeling—Anger.
Intention—To express anger in a constructive way.
Expression—"Honey, when I saw you with Marlene to-
night, I felt angry because it seemed you wanted to
be with her more than with me."

As I watch couples communicate I pick up a lot of unawareness of intention. The marriage of one couple I know is unlikely to survive the husband's infidelity because the wife is not aware of her intention to punish him for it.

Marge says that she wants to save her marriage in spite of two infidelities by her husband, Rick, in ten years. Rick is trying very hard to rebuild Marge's sense of security, but not a week goes by that Marge doesn't throw a verbal barb at Rick for his infidelities. Rick says, "Sometimes I wonder if I've made the right decision to stay with Marge. Every time I hear her sarcasm my stomach goes into a knot."

Marge says, "I don't know why I do it. Maybe I'm still angry at Rick." I think she is. Not only is she angry, she acts as if she wants to punish him.

It may seem as if she has a perfect right to be angry, but if she wants to save her marriage, she has to decide (her intention) if she wants to punish Rick with her sarcasm or deal with her anger in a more constructive way.

Seeing a counselor by herself would be helpful. There are therapeutic ways of getting out anger and closing "unfinished business." Or, she could get together with a close girl friend and vent her anger by talking about it. Often, hearing yourself express your feelings and knowing that someone understands and sympathizes helps get the poison out. But one thing is sure. She can't continue to punish Rick and rebuild her marriage at the same time.

We must be aware that negative feelings are often translated into an *intention* to hurt the person we're angry at. If we're not aware, we will thwart good communication.

*Lack of Awareness.* Lack of awareness has been a major problem in good communication between Andy and me. We have not been totally aware of what's going on in each other.

Even as I was working on this chapter we had another experience, and again, it was at a restaurant (we like to eat). We had been out for the evening, and Andy had taken me and our youngest son, Jonathan, to a restaurant. After Jon and I ordered, Andy just ordered something to drink.

I was surprised that he wasn't going to eat, and as I found out later, it came across to Andy as annoyance. He felt that I was annoyed that he wasn't going to eat, and that annoyed him. He felt, "Why should I have to eat when I don't want to?"

My real feelings were that I was comfortable with the idea of eating out if *he* wanted to. But I have a hard time saying what I want. I tend to go along with what others want and not insist on having my wishes considered.

We talked about this later, and I came to realize that Andy doesn't always know what I want because I cover it up so well. I'm really afraid to state what I want because the pain of being turned down is too great a risk. So I play it safe. I try to figure out what others want. Or I try to get others to suggest doing what I want to do. Or I say that it doesn't matter what we do.

But in spite of our failures, there's a bright side to it all. Later, after we ate and talked about my reaction to his not eating, Andy told me, "Tell me what you want. I want to please you, but I can't unless I know." I tucked that away for future reference, but forgot about it.

The next day I was thinking how drab the kitchen looked. I sure would like to have it remodeled. So I said to Andy, "You're going to kill me, but do you know what I'm thinking?" When I told him what I wanted to do he was very matter-of-fact and said, "Great, let's give it some thought." We've been doing more than thinking. Today we went out and looked at new kitchens!

I really feel sad when I realize that I've denied my own wishes a lot over the years simply because I've been afraid to make people aware of how I feel and what I want. Rather than risk being turned down, I've kept my mouth shut and have gone along with others.

*Summary.* Now what have we seen in this chapter? Just this. Though none of us perfectly exercises total awareness, that's a goal to strive for. We need to know five things about each other.

> Our senses—What are we each experiencing with our five senses?
>
> Our interpretations—What interpretations are we giving to the things we sense? Are these interpretations correct?
>
> Our feelings—What are we feeling about those things we sense, and the interpretations we give them?
>
> Our intention—What do we intend to say or do about our senses, interpretations, and feelings?
>
> Our expressions—Are we expressing ourselves with complete awareness of our senses, interpretations, feelings, and intentions?

*11*

# The Eight Issues
# We Need To Talk About

### —By André

MARRIAGE AND FAMILY THERAPISTS are often asked, "What are the major issues that people fight over? Are they money, sex, in-laws, child rearing, or what?"

All of these are major problems. But I prefer to look at the issues in terms of the "emotional stakes" that are involved. People argue over a variety of things but are not always aware of the larger psychological climate and the feelings that relatively innocent topics touch.

For example, a wife may become very emotional over what appears on the surface as rather minor things. For example, it may seem to her that her husband tends to come home from work when he's ready. He also pursues his own activities as he pleases without much attention to her wants. He lives his life quite independently of her. He asks himself if this is enough to get emotional over? Yes, if we see the real issue for what it is: centricity.

She is asking the question, "Am I important?" The question of her importance to her husband carries big emotional stakes, so big that she often wonders, "If I'm really not important to him, why should I stay in this marriage?"

I don't mean to imply that the relationship is the only thing that we need to talk about. Sometimes we need to discuss a certain *topic*, sometimes *personal* matters that concern someone else, and other times the discussion centers on the *relationship* of the husband and wife. But the eight issues in this chapter are all related to the husband/wife *relationship*. This is where we have our greatest difficulty in communication.

## THE ISSUES

George Bach and Yetta Bernhard discuss "psychological issues" in their book *Aggression Lab*.[1] They suggest that there are at least eight issues that carry high emotional stakes for couples who would communicate effectively. They are *distance, power struggle, trust, self-identity, sex, centricity, unrealistic illusions and expectations,* and *territorial aggression*. It's amazing what a different perspective we gain when we see the issues in terms of the "emotional stakes." Let's take a look at each of these issues and see what we can discover.

*Distance.* Every couple needs to establish a distance they feel comfortable with. This involves both *physical closeness* and *how much time* is spent together. Most couples don't find too much problem with actual physical closeness, though this can be a problem. A wife may want cuddling from her husband, but when he always takes her affection as an invitation to sex, she may become irritated. Women can distinguish between the need to be cuddled and the need for sex, though sometimes these needs go together.

More frequently, problems arise over how much closeness they have or how much time they have together. Often, a wife will complain that she doesn't have enough time with her husband. He, on the other hand, may complain that he doesn't have enough time for himself and his interests. And when he tries to take this time, his wife feels rejected. Feeling cut out, she may attempt to narrow the distance by trying to get closer to her husband. He may respond to that move by stepping up his bid for privacy until a vicious circle of negative reinforcement sets in—each does something to provoke a negative response in the other.

One wife complained to me that her husband never wanted to do things with her. To that he replied, "I feel as if she's smothering me. I need some time for myself." The issue was not that her husband didn't love her—something that could have been argued endlessly. The issue was distance comfortable to both. Here's where both can win. The wife gives her husband comfortable distance when he needs it in exchange for times of closeness that she needs.

I should not make it sound, however, that the wife is always the close-binding one. In my counseling practice I frequently run into the possessive male whose primary problem is his wife's desire for activity apart from him—both in work and play. He tends to regard her as a possession that ought to stay put at home. And when she doesn't stay put, he feels insecure. He likes all his possessions in their place so he can feel free to do what he wishes.

One of the notable things about this kind of male is that he really doesn't want his wife home so he can be with her. Often, when she does stay home, he will go out by himself or with his friends without her. This is why I say that he treats her like a possession—a thing—so that, when it's in its place, he can feel secure in going about his own business.

The issue of distance is one that must be settled to the satisfaction of each. Couples may try arm-twisting methods, complete with appropriate quotations from Scripture (men are usually guilty of using the "submission" passages), but this is no way to pursue a solution. Each must understand the other's needs. Each needs to send "I" messages on the subject and "active-listen." Only then will each discover what the other feels is a comfortable proximity. Once you discover that, you're in a position to propose a change that will work.

*Power Struggle.* The second issue that creates lots of problems in communication is "power struggle." This issue has to do with who calls the shots in the marriage. Does the husband always make the decisions or does the wife have a clearly defined area of responsibility in which she may make decisions? Who defines situations? For example, was the husband flirtatious with Marlene at the party as his wife claims, or was he merely being sociable as he claims? Is the situation always as he sees it, or is she allowed to disagree and define the situation differently—and have the definition stick? For example, when he socializes with his business friends, is it business as he claims or pleasure as she claims?

Often, when couples argue over everything and anything, they should consider the possibility that neither can tolerate the idea of giving in to the other. The notable thing about a power struggle is not *what* a couple argues over. It's that they seem to argue over *everything.* If there is a possibility for a difference of opinion, they will find it.

In a marriage of equals there should be a mutual respect and balance where each shares the responsibility of defining the situation. Let me give several examples. Is the husband thoughtless [the wife's definition] or is the wife too sensitive [the husband's definition]? Is their daughter rebellious and disobedient [the wife's definition] or just a normal teenager [the husband's definition]? In reality *both* may be wrong, or there may be some truth in the way each defines the situation. But is each willing to explore the other's definition of the situation?

Christian couples who don't have a balanced view of the headship of the husband will often put the wife in the position where she is to have no opinion, and her view is never the correct view—unless it happens to agree with her husband's. Christian women who labor under a tyrannical view of headship often find themselves in conflict with what they are told by the husband and what they believe to be true.

If Ephesians 5:22–33 and First Peter 3:1–7 are properly

applied there need be no power struggle. God has called the woman to be a helper "suitable" for her husband (Gen. 2:18). The word translated "suitable" quite literally means "counterpart." This suggests that the woman is an equal of a different kind. As an equal in grace she is able to bring something of equal value to the relationship.

The headship of the husband does not exclude the wisdom and talent of the wife. Indeed, the husband who values his wife as his counterpart and fellow-heir will value her perspective. The woman described in Proverbs 31:10–31 is a vigorous, talented woman who engages in her own business enterprise. To be sure, it's for the benefit of the family. But she is a person in her own right.

Why, then, do couples engage in power struggle? They must honestly examine what's going on inside themselves. Is the husband still battling with an unresolved power struggle with his mother or some other significant female of the past which he continues with his wife? Is the wife still struggling with an unresolved power struggle with her father or some other significant male of the past which she still carries on with her husband?

Often the issue of self-worth is at stake. The feeling is, "If I give in to him [or her] my self-worth will take a crushing blow. I will be admitting that he/she is right and I'm wrong."

*Trust.* The third issue is trust. Can a couple expose feelings to each other, or otherwise make themselves vulnerable, without fear of being hurt?

A couple that had argued endlessly over how much the husband should drink came to see that the issue was a deep fear in the wife that her husband would hurt her through some irresponsible act due to his drinking. One drink was enough to trigger her fear. She never knew how many more drinks would follow—and lay her open to danger.

Couples often refuse to share deep feelings for fear of hurt. The husband who wants sexual relations with his wife may be

afraid to ask because he is afraid of being denied. When he is
denied he feels demasculinized and vulnerable. He has sexual
feelings that need to be relieved, but if his wife denies him, she
puts him in the position of needing sex but of having no acceptable outlet for it. Again, this can lead to a circle of negative reinforcement. He is afraid to ask because he can't trust
her; she gets the impression that he has no sexual need because he doesn't ask! In such a case the issue needs to be
identified. The husband may say, "Honey, I am in a bind.
There are times when I want very much to have sexual relations with you, but I'm afraid to ask. I'm afraid that if I ask,
you may say no, and that will leave me feeling hurt and vulnerable. I would feel that my masculinity was put down and
vulnerable because I need sex, but I have nowhere to go."

*Self-Identity.* The fourth issue is "defense of self-identity."
This becomes an issue when one spouse tries to get the other
to play a role that seems foreign or unnatural. Often romantic
ideals are established in courtship, and though they are un-
real, each spouse tries to live up to them until the strain becomes unbearable. They then fall into arguing about the
things they don't want to do rather than dealing with the real
issue—self-identity. It is being defended, and so we have
conflict over it.

For example, a man may choose a woman to be his wife
because she appears to be a good socializer. She seems to love
parties and people. He feels that she will make the ideal hostess for his business friends. What he doesn't know is that this
role is really foreign to her. She appears to be the life of the
party in their courtship because she knows that this is what he
wants. She actually colludes with him in establishing a false
identity and a foreign role.

After years of grimly suffering through entertaining his
business friends and having many fights over his expectations
of her as a hostess, it finally comes out that she really does not
feel comfortable in this role. The issue is not, "Who will be

entertained, where, when, and how." The issue is that she is cast in the foreign role of the perfect hostess who loves parties.

I have seen this tragedy unfold in the homes of ministers and professional men such as doctors and lawyers. A woman loves a man who is planning to go into a very demanding profession. She loves him so much that she convinces herself that she will do anything for his love. If it requires socializing or many hours of separation, which is foreign to her, she may collude with her man in assuming a foreign role of socializer and strong, independent woman who can make it when her husband isn't around. After the years pass and the electric experience of courtship is a dim memory, she finds herself trapped in a role foreign to her with no way out. The way out is to identify the issue of self-identity and communicate for change.

*Sex.* Sex is an issue that also carries high emotional stakes but is often obscured as the real issue. Questions such as, "What kind of sex, how often, and under what conditions?" are highly relevant.

The spouse who wants to avoid sexual encounter may make excuses. The wife, for example, may become very busy with the children, attentive to their needs and home and chauffeuring them unnecessarily, so she can avoid her husband. At night or at other moments when the children are not around she may use the excuse of exhaustion. Whenever I hear a mother angrily justify the amount of time she spends on her children at the exclusion of all else, even her husband, I have a hunch that she's using them to avoid something—or someone. If she's trying to avoid her husband, then that's what they need to talk about.

Wives are not the only ones who try to avoid sex, however. Sometimes a husband may spend extra hours on the job and then come home too exhausted for sex. When the wife complains, he then pulls a guilt manipulation. He says, "Here I work myself to exhaustion to give you all the things you want, and all I get is nagging."

One problem I often encounter with Christian couples is in the kind of sex-play they will engage in. Sometimes the husband wants the wife to wear erotic garments and engage in sex play that she regards as distasteful. This often leads to her turning him off. She feels as if he's treating her like a Playboy bunny.

If the husband has a warped view of Christian headship he may quote First Corinthians 7:1–5 and tell her that it's her duty to do as he says. But if she has sex under these conditions she's ripe for a psychological reaction.

Husbands who come on like this need to be reminded that Christian husbands are to treat their wives differently than the pagans treat their wives. Paul says that sexually they are to possess the wife in "sanctification and honor" and not as the pagans did (1 Thess. 4:1–5). The word "sanctification" means "set apart as that which is holy." In this sense I think it has to do with making the wife feel special and treating her with the kind of deference that one does with someone special.

"Honor" is the same word used in First Peter 3:7 where the husband is told to assign honor to his wife as his equal, his fellow-heir of the grace of life. He hardly can treat her as a thing, a sex object, when he approaches her with this attitude.

I don't mean to imply that sex for Christians can't be fun and innovative. All I'm saying is that the husband's attitude toward his wife is all-important.

*Centricity.* Of all the issues I run into in counseling, centricity creates more problems than any other. This issue asks the question, "Am I important?" The husband who seems to have time and energy for everyone and everything other than his wife raises this question in her mind. They may argue endlessly over how he spends his time, money, and energy, but these are not the issues. The issue is that he behaves in such a way as to make his wife feel that she's low on his list of priorities.

Take, for example, the husband who is repeatedly late for

supper. His wife, attempting to fulfill her role, has a tasty supper prepared at the usual time, and he doesn't show up. An hour later, when he does show up, he acts totally indifferent about the ruined supper. When asked why he's late, he casually explains that he stopped off at his favorite pro shop on the way home, and time got away from him. It seems that he just couldn't decide what tennis racket was right for him.

That kind of thoughtlessness is bad enough, but suppose he acts as if the tennis racket is the biggest thing in his life. Tennis is always getting between him and his wife. She can't watch what she wants on TV because he has to watch Bjorn Borg. Or he can't go to his wife's favorite symphony with her because he and his buddy have planned a tennis match.

The issues they argue over aren't really the dried-out rump roast or the relative merits of symphonic music and tennis. The issue to the wife is this: "I don't feel as if I'm important enough to you for you to want to be with me—either for supper or to do with me the things I like to do."

Husbands aren't the only offenders, however. Wives raise the same question in the minds of the husbands. And the problem may be more difficult to spot when her focus is on good things such as homemaking and mothering.

Some wives are so busy trying to be good homemakers that the husband feels the house is more important than he. One husband told me, "I hate to come home at night. She has spent all day tidying up the house, and when I walk in, if I leave one thing out of place, she nails me. I realize that I should keep my things picked up, but enough is enough. I'm even afraid to get up and go to the bathroom during the night because I'm sure I'll come back and find that she has made the bed.

"And the children—everything is for the children. It doesn't seem to matter what *I* want. We must be very good parents, ever attentive to the wants and needs of the children. I think she's ruining them, being at their beck and call every moment. And all this in the name of being a good parent. Well, she can have her lovely house and her lovely children, but she can count me out. I know when I'm not wanted!"

The sad thing about this case is that the wife in question would not see that the issue was centricity. She was determined that her "selfish" husband would not keep her from being a good mother and homemaker.

*Unrealistic Illusions and Expectations.* This issue often goes hand in hand with the issue of self-identity. The husband may place on the wife expectations that are disappointed because she feels, "This just isn't me."

I think a lot of problems that pastors and their wives have with each other are over this issue. Sometimes the man who enters the pastorate has certain unspoken expectations of his wife. And sometimes the church has the same expectations. But she, being unaware of these expectations, pursues her work as wife, mother, and homemaker, quite unaware that she is not living up to her husband's or congregation's idea of what a good pastor's wife ought to be doing—such as playing the organ, teaching a Bible study, acting as Chairman of the Ladies' Missionary Society, or whatever.

When those expectations are revealed (often in a very tense atmosphere) she feels, "Wait a minute. That just isn't me [defense of self-identity]. Why didn't you tell me that this was the name of the game before I got into it?"

I know of a pastor and his wife who tried to anticipate this problem before they accepted the call to a church. They made it clear to the church that they felt a pastor's wife was first and foremost just that—the pastor's wife, and not an assistant pastor. She would do no more or no less than any other dedicated Christian woman in the church.

Everyone said he understood, but it didn't work that way. In the six years they were at that church, some of the women repeatedly called the wife's attention to all the things the former pastor's wife did that she was not doing.

*Territorial Aggression.* The eighth issue is "territorial aggression." The animal kingdom demonstrates this phenomenon well. Each animal has his own "turf"—that piece of property that is his, and no other animal better step on his turf! Human beings also have their turf. It may be living space in the house, such as the husband's study, or it may be symbolic turf and symbolic aggression. For example, who drives the car when the husband and wife travel together? If she drives, does he feel that she is trespassing where she shouldn't? When they are in the car together, does he feel that his place is at the wheel? Likewise, "backseat driving" by the wife may be felt to be a form of territorial aggression by the husband. When she tells him how to drive he may feel that she is intruding on his turf.

The wife also has her turf. She may feel that the kitchen or the laundry room is her turf. She may appear to get unreasonably angry when her husband or children mess things up, or barge in when she is working in these rooms. She may feel a personal attack because this is her turf. Generally, women are very sensitive about the appearance of their homes. Society tends to regard the home as the woman's turf, and therefore, how it looks is of major concern to her. She will feel, "My friends' view of me is conditioned by how my house looks. Husband and children, you better not leave it a mess!"

I'll always remember one couple who instantly resolved a terrible conflict the moment they saw this was the problem. Jim and Linda both worked outside the home, so when Jim had a day off, he thought he'd do something nice for Linda. She always seemed to feel terribly responsible for keeping the kitchen clean and good meals on the table. So he thought he'd share her burden.

The kitchen looked cluttered to him and not very efficient (he's an industrial efficiency expert by profession). He thought it needed rearranging and sprucing up.

He was quite proud of his efforts when he finished several hours later. Linda would be delighted, so he thought, and maybe she'd also appreciate his fixing supper. He prepared a fine supper and timed it perfectly so it would be ready when Linda walked in.

At zero hour, when she walked in, he expected to be smothered with kisses for his thoughtfulness. Instead, Linda did a double-take and gave him a peck on the cheek. She was less than enthusiastic about his arrangement of the kitchen.

Jim figured she must have had a bad day. So he got on with the dinner. She acted strangely when he sat her down and served dinner. Where were the smiles and accolades?

As they ate in silence, Jim tried to figure out what was wrong. He soon found out.

Linda (playing with a vegetable on her plate): "What's this?"

Jim (tentatively): "A new recipe for zucchini."

Linda (unenthusiastically): "Oh." (Pushing the zucchini aside and trying a few bits of the roast, she continued): "The roast sure is tough and dry."

That was it! Enough was enough! Jim uncorked! The battle that followed made Hitler's invasion of Poland look like an exercise in human decency. Never did they fight like that!

According to Linda, everything was wrong with the kitchen, and the meal wasn't fit for hogs. And according to Jim, never did he dream that he was married to such an ingrate. Every real and imagined hurt over fifteen years of marriage roared down on them like a tornado.

Of course the issue was territorial aggression. Though he was well-meaning, Jim had intruded on Linda's turf.

Our turf has a lot to do with our sense of identity and our role in marriage. When someone trespasses it is a very personal matter. And when this is complicated by feelings of low self-worth, watch out!

Linda felt that Jim was implying she was not doing "her job" of homemaking to his satisfaction. In her mind he was saying. "Let me show you how it ought to be done."

This was not Jim's intention. And here is a classic example of a breakdown in communication because of an inadequate understanding of feelings and intentions.

I'm happy to say that they made peace. Understanding that the issue was territorial aggression, they were able to put things in their proper perspective. People who want to make their marriage work usually respond to such insights.

## DEADLY COMBINATIONS OF ISSUES

Often, the issues that create problems in marriage are not just single issues. Understanding what we need to talk about can be complicated by a deadly combination of issues.

*Sex and Trust.* Problems relating to sex often combine with lack of trust. Husbands and wives are vulnerable when they express themselves sexually and must be able to trust each other with this sensitive area of their personhood. It's not unusual, for example, for a woman to find it difficult to be open to her husband sexually when he has been guilty of infidelity. But women are not the only ones to suffer from this deadly combination.

A client with impotency was referred to me by a doctor because the problem was not physical. The only other explanation was psychological. As we talked about the problem I explained to him that any time a man carries anger or fear into the bedroom he will have this kind of problem.

After much soul searching he identified the trouble. With tears he spilled it out.

"In all the years I've been married I've supposed that if my wife didn't meet my sexual needs I'd just leave her and find someone else. Now after twenty-five years of marriage I've come to realize that I love her so much I could never leave her—even for sex with someone else. Suddenly I felt extremely vulnerable to her. She is the only woman I will ever love—sexually or otherwise.

"When that hit me, it seemed as though she had a power over me that she never had before. That's good news and bad

news. It's good because it says something about her importance to me. But it's bad because it makes me feel so vulnerable. That's the fear I'm carrying into the bedroom."

When his wife learned that this was his problem, she
became a soft, warm, accepting creature. She gave him the
clear message that he didn't *have to* perform sexually. She was
willing to follow his lead and do whatever he wanted to do.
She was so deeply touched by his love for her that it relieved
him of his fear—and his problem.

*Power Struggle and Unrealistic Expectations.* In the first chapter I told the story of Hank and Betty. Theirs was a case of a
deadly combination of power struggle and unrealistic expectations. Hank, because of his view of headship, had some expectations of Betty that she felt were unrealistic. He expected her
to give him rubber-stamp approval of everything he did. If he
didn't feel like going to work, she was to go along with it. If he
wanted her to pick up the children at any hour, day or night,
and go off with him wherever he wanted to go, she was to do it.
If they were working out in the yard and he wanted a hammer,
he felt he should be able to tell her to run down to the tool shed
and get it. In fact, that was one of the things that made her
decide she wasn't going to let him treat her like his slave. He
told her to get him a hammer, and she told him to get it
himself!

This resulted in a power struggle. Because of his unrealistic expectations of her (she was to be his obedient slave) she
decided that she was going to stand and fight him. The power
struggle took the form of her resisting him in every way she
knew how. She would not yield in any way. This, of course,
was bound to be a destructive experience for both of them. But
by eliminating the unrealistic expectations they were able to
eliminate the need for the power struggle.

*Summary.* Here, then are the eight issues we need to talk
about: *distance, power struggle, trust, self-identity, sex, centricity,*

*unrealistic illusions and expectations,* and *territorial aggression.* If you get the feeling that you really don't know what the problem seems to be in your communication, stop and see if any of these issues might be the real problem, and if not a single issue, perhaps a combination of them. One way to do this is to write a "State of the Union" message to each other—the subject of the next chapter.

# "State of the Union" Message

## —BY ANDRÉ

SOMEONE ONCE SAID, "An unexamined life is hardly worth living." The same may be true of marriage. This chapter suggests a practical way to examine the unexamined marriage. It's done with a "state of the union" message.

A "state of the union" message is a non-threatening, non-attacking way in which husbands and wives can tell each other how they feel about the marriage.[1] It is a statement about each of the eight issues described in the previous chapter. Alone and separately, the husband and wife meditate on each of the eight issues to determine how each feels about them. These feelings are stated in writing. No accusations or demands are to be made. Questions must be handled carefully. They should express a need for information that may be given in a pow-wow later. This is a prearranged agreement to talk about a specific agenda at a specific time. Sometimes the statements may be positive. Sometimes they will be negative. Sometimes mixed feelings are expressed concerning trends in the marriage.

For example, a wife writing on the issue of centricity may state a growing concern over her husband's spending more and more time away from her. She may ask for a pow-wow at a later time, but she is not to find fault with him about it while she's writing her message.

Couples will find writing their messages less threatening than delivering them face to face. After writing their messages, they should exchange them and read them privately. If anger, hurt, or resentment result from what is read, they should cool off and set a date to talk about it.

Some couples avoid this exercise simply because they are afraid of what they'll find out about their marriage. One woman said, "I have a pretty good marriage. Why should I risk disrupting it with something like this?"

I feel uneasy about that outlook. Couples who are growing together often disrupt the status-quo in order to provide more room for growth. I question how good a marriage is where the couple is unwilling to say how they feel about it. The marriage may be tolerable, but God wants more than a tolerable marriage.

A "state of the union" message may be given periodically (such as quarterly) if the couple agrees to it and will discipline themselves to do it. Or it may be given whenever one or the other feels the need to evaluate the relationship.

## A HUSBAND'S "STATE OF THE UNION" MESSAGE

Here's an example of a husband's "state of the union" message. I have pieced together several such messages from my own life and from others in order to illustrate each issue most effectively and to protect the privacy of those who have been willing to be open to each other and to me.

Remember the procedure. Each of the eight issues described in the previous chapter are to be discussed. There are to be no accusations or demands—only statements that are designed to explain what each is feeling.

*Distance.* "I feel comfortable about the distance we have. There's enough togetherness that I feel fulfilled by your friendship and companionship but also enough distance so I can pursue my work and interests.

"Sometimes I worry, though, that you want more time together. I'm afraid that you will take the pursuit of my own interests as rejection. I need you to keep me informed about your needs for closeness if you feel things are out of balance there."

*Power Struggle.* "Power struggle has never been one of our problems. I hope this isn't because I have tended to be dominant and you submissive. I worry that sometimes you go along with what I think and what I want because you're not comfortable about expressing your wants. I would rest easier if I knew that you would speak up if your wants or your view of things differs from mine."

*Trust.* "This issue touches two areas of our relationship. One is communication and the other sex.

"The communication issue is becoming less and less of a problem though sometimes I still have difficulty. My problem is this. Sometimes when we have a different view of things I'm afraid to get into that differentness because I may get cut down for having a view different from yours. It doesn't happen so much any more, but occasionally I get zinged with a sarcastic remark that infers I think I'm an authority on the subject.

"Perhaps I'm really guilty of sounding authoritative. If I am, I need to know—in a non-attacking way.

"Another area where trust may enter in has to do with your sharing your real thoughts and feelings with me. I feel much better about this now than I used to. But I guess what I'm saying is that I count on you to tell me what you're really thinking and feeling.

"Sometimes I pick up negative vibes, and I don't k⸢
what they are about. Then I tend to imagine the worst⸜
to have guilt feelings when that would happen a⸢

'What have I done now?' I don't do that so much any more. But when I pick up negative vibes and don't know what they're about, I still feel uneasy.

"Concerning trust and sex, I'll say more on that when I get to those issues. For now I'll simply say that sexually I feel very vulnerable to you. I just need you to know that's a very sensitive area in my ego right now, and I need to feel secure with you about it."

*Self-Identity.* "I feel pretty good about who I am. I perceive myself as an intense, competitive person. I like a certain amount of vigorous activity, and I feel good about the shape I'm in. I'm really in better shape now as a middle-aged man than I was when I was in high school.

"Sometimes I feel annoyance from you over my diet and physical conditioning. I'm afraid that you take this as an indirect message that you ought to diet and exercise. I can honestly say that this is not my intention. Or, if you don't feel as if it's a message to you, maybe you feel that I'm trying to impress other women.

"I can honestly say that I'm doing this for me. I don't feel as if I'm pushing fifty when I know that I'm in better shape than I was thirty-five years ago. I do think, however, that this is a symptom of mid-life male crisis. But can you understand what I mean when I say that I'm doing this for me?

"I have a hunch, too, that my physical fitness kick may have some relation to my feelings about sex. I think it may be either sublimation or compensation. For more about that, see my comments on sex.

"At any rate, please indulge my physical fitness routine. As middle-age behavior goes, it's a lot less of a problem than ʼinking or chasing women."

the com "Under the issue of self-identity I said that I suspect my physical fitness drive may be traced to sexual ublimation, or both. Let me explain.

"Over the past year I've noticed a marked change in my sex drive and my attitude toward sex. It no longer is the big thing it once was from my teen years on up.

"Rather than alarm me, this change has made me feel good. I feel more in control of myself sexually. Also, I feel that it more approximates your sex drive, bringing this dimension of our relationship more into balance.

"I think the reason for this change is more psychological than physical. Three things prompt that opinion.

"First, I am alarmed and dismayed at the marriages around us that are going under because of the husband's infidelity. And it's not just the marriages going under. The incredible pain I've seen is just terrible. It's like a plague that I don't want to get.

"Second, and this is closely related to the first, I am happy with our relationship. We have so many good things going for us I don't want any mid-life male stupidity to ruin things. No woman is worth the trade.

"Third, I feel that much of our sex in times past has been because I have wanted it. This may not be your perspective, but that's where I'm coming from. I want you to want me sexually. It strikes me as erotic that you should want sexual relations more than I.

"This brings me to compensation and/or sublimation. I don't know which fits. I don't know if I'm compensating for a reduction in sex drive with a drive for physical fitness or if I really do have strong sexual feelings driven underground by fear—feelings that are being sublimated by strenuous activity. I'll keep you up-to-date on any new insights I get.

"A major concern I have in this is that I don't neglect you sexually. I'm trusting you to be candid about your sexual needs.

"That prompts another thought. I wonder if I'm waiting for you to take the sexual initiative? I really don't know. I did say that it strikes me as erotic that your desire for me should be stronger than mine for you. I guess I need a psychologist to figure that one out! That prompts me to add this. If this should become a problem we can't solve, I'm open to sexual or marraige counseling."

*Centricity.* "I feel very important to you. If there ever has been a problem in this area I think that I've been too important to you. Please understand that I don't resent it. You know I play the role of protector, defender, and supporter too well! It's just that I don't think that it's healthy for me to be the only source of your physical and emotional support.

"You have changed in this regard over the years, and I've been glad for the change. I think you have begun to rely more on yourself and others.

"I'm particularly glad for your growing self-reliance. It seems to make you less vulnerable to the hurts that others deal you. Also, I often think that if I die before you, I would like to die with the assurance that you can take care of yourself and that I'm not doing you dirty by dying and leaving you without a protector.

"Lessening your dependence on me also has given me more breathing room. I've been able to get in touch more with what I want. I find that I'm able to pursue more of my own interests without worry or guilt over leaving you in the lurch. This doesn't mean that your increased self-reliance will mean more distance from me. It just makes our relationship easier."

*Unrealistic Illusions and Expectations.* "This issue doesn't present any problem to me. I don't think I have any unrealistic expectations of you. You'll have to tell me if I do. As far as your expectations of me—I don't feel you do. If anything, I need to know that I'm fulfilling your expectations of me. As I have said under other issues, I need to know what you think and feel."

*Territorial Aggression.* "I don't feel that you're invading any of 'my turf.' That may be either because I'm not conscious of my turf or because you're not the aggressive type. I think that the latter is the reason.

"This brings me again to a theme that I've mentioned throughout. I need to know what your needs are, whether they're closeness, distance, time, money, sex, or what. I'm coming to understand that it's a new thing for you to get in touch with what you want and feel okay about it. All I'm asking is that you do two things. Tell me what you want, and tell me how important it is to you. I know what I want. And the only way I have of comparing our wants is for you to tell me."

## A WIFE'S "STATE OF THE UNION" MESSAGE

The wife may write her first "state of the union" message without the information her husband has provided in his. But of course after she reads his message, her next one should clear up questions he has about her.

Her message should cover the same eight issues her husband covers.

It should be without accusation or demand, though she may ask for a pow-wow when she needs information. Here's how her message may go.

*Distance.* "I generally feel pretty good about the balance we have between our times together and our times apart. I don't know that I want more time with you. But when I make a suggestion about doing something together that you may not want to do, it doesn't help for me to hear that it's okay if I do it by myself. Usually, when I want to do something with you, there's a special attraction in doing it together. It's something I want to share with you.

"Sometimes I think I'm a bit jealous over your wide variety of interests. You seem to be able to entertain yourself without much trouble. I think that the development of my interests in my childhood was thwarted, and as a result, I don't always know what I want to do."

*Power Struggle.* "I generally agree that power struggle has not been one of our problems. But I think sometimes I have resisted you in a passive way. Because of changes in you in recent years I have begun to feel freer about expressing myself. I used to be fearful that if I expressed a point of view different from yours, you would bulldoze me. This is becoming less of a problem. I feel as if I'm being heard and that my point of view and needs are being respected. I still need to watch out for my passive resistance, however."

*Trust.* "I don't have any major problem in this area. I generally feel secure with you.

"Sometimes I have problems when I see women give you the eye. But I don't think it's so much a lack of trusting you as anger at someone giving you the once-over.

"You said that you have a problem trusting me to say what I really feel, especially when you pick up negative vibes and don't know what they're about. I sometimes really am not aware that I'm giving negative vibes, or if I am feeling negative, I'm not always aware of what it's about. I'm open to having you check it out when you pick up negative vibes from me."

*Self-Identity.* "I have a bit of a problem here—not so much with you but with others. And when it spills over into our relationship and poisons it, I realize that I need to tell you what's going on. Again, the problem is awareness. I'm not always aware that my self-identity has taken a beating until I begin to talk sarcastically.

"I think my biggest problem is with the feminists who tell me that I ought to be getting into a career and doing something 'more meaningful' with my life. I'm perfectly happy to make a home for you, read, watch TV, and enjoy moments of solitude. But then I run into some female who is running off in four directions at once who asks me, 'And what activities are you involved in?' I want to tell her, 'As few as possible.' Why can't they just let me be me? Why do I have to have a 'cause' or be demonstrating with placards?

"I need your assurance that you don't feel this way. I'd like to feel better about myself being just as I am.

"About your concern over my reaction to your physical fitness kick, let me say this. It used to bother me. I think it was more jealousy than anything else—your ability to discipline yourself. This seemed to hook into what people were telling me about my need to get involved and do something meaningful. Just seeing you diet and exercise seemed to reinforce the message. So I was angry at your reinforcing their message, and jealous too!"

*Sex.* "I generally feel good about our sexual relations. I have wondered about your apparent disinterest. I feel more sexually inclined when we are away from home doing something special together. Home is where work and responsibility are. When we're traveling the atmosphere seems more romantic and conducive to love-making. I'd like to be able to tell you more about myself sexually, but perhaps this is another area of my feelings that I've not been too aware of.

"One thing that does come to mind is that I feel we're building a new relationship. For many years our relationship was strained. I felt dominated and bullied by you so I turned off sexually. Now that we are growing closer together I find that my sexual feelings toward you are changing too. As I sort out my feelings, I'll keep you informed."

*Centricity.* "This issue needs some attention. I feel that I'm more important to you now than I was ten years ago, but sometimes I still think that you could get along quite well without me.

"I think part of the problem has to do with my limited interests. You have lots of things you can enjoy without me, and I think I'm a bit jealous over that. Then I feel guilty because I don't want to be a spoil-sport.

"Part of the problem is my own 'mid-life crisis.' You're just coming into your prime in your work. But what's happened to me? I've worked myself out of a job I've had for thirty years—the job of mothering and homemaking. There's only so much homemaking I can do now for the two of us. So, with all the children gone from the nest, you're the only one left to spend my attentions on.

"I'm glad that you feel I'm becoming more self-reliant. It does worry me though that you'll take that as a signal to spend more time on your interests and less on me.

"Please understand that I too am feeling vulnerable. While I've worked myself out of a job, my husband has reached the acme of his profession. You have time and money to pursue your interests, and you have a lot of them. I have few. And even though I trust you, it seems that you are growing more attractive with age than I. I really need to know that I am important to you."

*Unrealistic Illusions and Expectations.* "I don't feel that your expectations of me are unrealistic. And my expectations of you are being fulfilled. My problem is with the expectations others have and how that poisons our relationship. When feminists tell me that I ought to do something 'more meaningful' than I'm doing, I wonder if I should and if you wouldn't be happier with a more active wife. And then when I see you so active yourself, I'm convinced that you would be happy with a more active woman.

"I realize that this is something I put on myself. I do need your assurance that I am meeting your expectations of me."

*Territorial Aggression.* "I don't feel that you're intruding on my turf. Sometimes when I see you tidy things up in the kitchen I wonder if you're displeased with my performance. But I don't mind your doing it. I don't think this has ever been a problem with us. And I don't think it's because I've been passive and have suffered from your aggression.

"In summary I feel good about our relationship. I need to talk more about self-identity and centricity. Perhaps we can have a pow-wow."

## COMMENT ON THE MESSAGES

You will note that these messages do not make demands for change but do ask for communication in areas of doubt. They are a good example of an on-going "I" message—here's where I am; I need to know where you are.

Remember, the first thing we're looking for is understanding, not agreement. The state of the union message is an attempt to reveal self and to solicit the revelation of the spouse's innermost thoughts and feelings.

Another thing to note is that sometimes the writers are not totally clear about where they are on some of the issues. The husband's sexual feelings is one example. He is not holding back information. He simply doesn't know, but promises to keep his wife informed.

*Dealing With a "Threatened Spouse."* It's very likely that a husband or wife may feel too threatened to deal with all the issues in the "state of the union" message. Start, then, with the issues that are "safe" to write about. On the issues that are threatening, simply state why they are threatening to write about. For example they may reveal more about you than you're ready to reveal right now. Or they may be explosive issues. In such a case talk about why you don't want to reveal yourself. You may be afraid your spouse will hurt or ridicule you. He needs to know. You need to explore why the issue may be explosive. Such discussion can be very productive.

*How About Talking Instead of Writing?* Sometimes people are not good at putting their ideas on paper. Should they give a verbal "state of the union" message? No, not until they've had a lot of experience in sharing their feelings. Writing and reading is much less threatening than face to face confrontation. If you have trouble writing about your feelings, use a tape recorder. Get away by yourself and start talking. Then have your spouse listen to the tape alone.

A couple with a lot of experience in sharing will eventually give their "state of the union" message verbally and face to face. But for the beginner, a written or taped message is less threatening.

### CALLING A POW-WOW

Calling a pow-wow (p/w) is a way to build on the understanding begun in the state of the union messages. In a husband/wife p/w several guidelines are to be observed.

*Calling the Pow-Wow.* Whoever calls the p/w has a right to set the agenda. For example, the wife calls the p/w to talk about the issues of self-identity and centricity. The agenda may be changed only with her approval. If the husband wants to call his own p/w and set the agenda, he may. But observance of the rule will keep the purpose of the p/w from being thwarted.

*Timing.* The time for the p/w should be by mutual agreement. If the wife calls the p/w she may suggest a time and day. But they should agree on a specific time and even put it on their appointment calendar.

*Importance of Using Your Skills.* The skills of active-listening, sending "I" messages and shifting gears are to be employed. No attack or defense is permitted. The purpose is to share information.

*Time Limits.* Minimum and maximum time limits should be set. A minimum of ten to fifteen minutes and a maximum of one hour are reasonable. If the one who calls the p/w sees that more time is needed, an extension may be requested. But it should be done with mutual consent, or another time should be set to continue the discussion.

The p/w should be distinguished from communication for change. In a p/w we are simply looking for clarification of the state of the union message or more information about it. Communication for change follows a different format. This we see in the next chapter.

*Summary.* A state of the union message is a practical way to apply the skill of sending "I" messages. By doing it in writing, it is less threatening than a face-to-face discussion. Giving such a message is not easy. But it will help you keep up with changes that are going on with each other. A thoroughly examined marriage can be very worthwhile and a delightful experience.

# 13

# *Communicating for Change*

## —By André

THE PRACTICAL-MINDED COUPLE will be looking for a chapter in this book on "problem solving" or "negotiating differences." Every book on communication needs such a chapter. Well, this is it.

I call it "communicating for change," because "problem solving" seems to create an image of two people at odds with each other grimly going about the task of negotiating their differences through commercial-style bargains of the *quid pro quo* variety—"this for that."

Contracting is foreign to the thesis and spirit of this book. Couples who respect their differences and care about each other are able to talk about those differences in a spirit of good will. They can *unilaterally make changes simply because they care about each other*. The primary ingredients needed for such unilateral change are a respect for their differentness, a thorough understanding of the changes that are desired, and a desire to change and please both self and the other spouse.

Bach and Bernhard say this about contracts:

"Quid pro quo"—this for that—is the basis for legal contracts. In the business world contracts are based on the *exchange* of goods or services. Please note that in the fair fight system this kind of bargaining is *not* recommended. "Equality" is a commercial value rather than an intimate reality. What is "good for the goose" in a relationship is not necessarily what is "good for the gander."

Realistic intimacy flourishes better under conditions of coexistence of clearly differentiated individuals who know how to deal with their very real differences. . . . Togetherness in intimacy does not mean sameness. Consequently, the commercial definition of contracts does not apply in relationships. Unlike the business world which has money as a medium of exchange, human relationships have no way to compare and weigh the worth of behavior. We have found clinically that contracts based on the notion of bargaining—"I'll do this if you'll do that"—tend to have a much lower probability of being fulfilled than those contracts that are in the nature of a unilateral commitment—"I will do this for you because I wish to please you."[1]

## Premises of This Book

To help you understand what I propose in communication for change, let me list the premises this book is based on.

*Respect of Differentness.* Differentness can be exciting. Most people marry for complimentary reasons. Only when that differentness is declared bad, wrong, or unsuitable does the complimentarity become a problem. We need not think alike nor act alike in marriage in order for it to work and even be exciting. But we do need to understand the scope of that differentness. We need to be able, with accurate empathy, to enter into that other person's world of pain and pleasure and to hear it, see it, think it, and feel it as he or she does. This requires an openness, one with the other, and a trust in each other that the differentness will be respected.

Any attempt at change that does not fully fathom the differentness in each other will be mechanical. There will be no true understanding of the need for change, and, because of that, enduring change is unlikely.

*A Thorough Understanding of the Changes Desired.* The second premise is that when differences exist as a result of different-ness, a thorough understanding of the changes desired is needed. Remember, we are looking for understanding, not agreement. Those differences are to be shared in a non-attacking way through the use of "I" messages, active-listening, and shifting gears.

It's not easy to go through the process of saying or hearing painful things. Many couples would like to find a style of communication and method of change that is painless. But effective communication demands that we make constructive impact on each other. Impact that is not felt is not impact. Yes, we try to make it as non-attacking and painless as we can, but impact implies that you will feel *something*.

Effective communication for change cannot be painless, for it challenges the *status-quo*—a challenge that makes all of us nervous. We tend to hang on to the *status-quo,* no matter how unrewarding, because it is familiar and possibly safe.

Some contracts for change are an attempt to avoid the pain of discussing differences and desires. But we just cannot approach intimacy with a commercial or legal mentality.

I am not saying that all contracts are wrong. Learning contracts or contracts for specific tasks are possible to negotiate, but they are only adjuncts to change as a unilateral decision.[2] A unilateral decision simply means that I am willing to change because I want to please you, and not because I'm going to get something in return. Having a pleased spouse is reward enough!

*Desire to Change in Order to Please Self and Spouse.* One final premise has to do with this matter of pleasing. We need a thorough understanding of our differences and the changes that are being asked. But this must occur in a context of good-will where both want to make changes that will please both spouses.

I realize that when I encourage you to send "I" messages and active-listen that I'm asking you to open yourself to hearing things that are painful. But whether you feel damaged by what you hear, or if you find it a constructive step in the direction of change, will depend on the context you and your spouse have established. If it is a context of ill-will and you're on a "hurt hunt," it will be a damaging experience. If it is in a context of good-will, it will be painful but rewarding.

It's important to make these distinctions:

Good-will is interested in furthering the strength of the marriage.

Ill-will has no interest in furthering that bond.

Good-will sees you as a person with feelings that are to be respected.

Ill-will sees you as a "thing" to be used, or as an anonymous creature.

Without these three premises (respect of differentness, understanding of the changes desired, and willingness to please), communication for change will be impossible. You need to be able to express your desire for change in an understanding and receptive atmosphere. Communication for change that is attempted in an atmosphere of misunderstanding and distrust will not succeed. When that happens the issues that need to be addressed are misunderstanding and distrust.

## MAKING IMPACT FOR CHANGE

Let's suppose that you do have the proper atmosphere for change. How do you go about communicating for change? You must be able to make "impact" on your spouse. By that I mean that you must state in a straightforward and clear way what you would like to see changed, and specifically, what changes you want. You are levelling with your spouse about how you feel and what you want. Because it is done in an understanding and accepting atmosphere and in a non-attacking and non-defensive way, "impact" is not experienced as hostility.

In chapter 6 I described the Revolving Discussion Sequence. This method is a variation of it. Bach and Bernhard call it a "fair fight for change."[3]

I see eight steps in making impact for change: *Engagement, statement of the problem, feedback to the statement, request for change, feedback to the proposed change, response, rejection or acceptance,* and *planning the next engagement and closure.*

*Engagement.* If you wish to communicate for change your spouse must be willing to do so. Instead of jumping right in and talking to him about your need, you must ask him if he is willing to talk with you about the specific issue that bothers you. You may say, "Honey, I have a problem with the way we handle our son. Would you be willing to talk with me about it?"

He may accept, postpone, or reject talking with you about it. Or, he may want to talk about a different issue. You want to be careful, however, that rejection or the introduction of a different issue is not a sign of communication sabotage (see chapters 14 and 15).

My experience is that more husbands are closed to communication than their wives. They simply avoid talking about anything that might be painful. They tend to keep the discussion superficial.

If your husband refuses to engage in communication or ties up the communication in fruitless fights over what you "ought" to talk about, you have a communication saboteur on your hands. And, as I point out in chapters 14 and 15, the problem must be stated exactly that way—it is *sabotage.* You must not settle for some vague agreement that the two of you "just can't talk about your problems." You *can* if you approach it with respect of differentness, understanding, and a desire to please. But you can't if there's sabotage.

If your spouse wants to postpone the engagement, fine, but be sure to set a specific day and time to engage in your communication for change. Also, when you do engage, you may want to ask if you can follow the methodology described in this chapter. Explain that this methodology is designed to promote understanding and reduce the possibility of conflict.

*Statement of Your Problem.* Following the principles given in chapter 8, state your problem in terms of an "I" message. Remember, "I" messages involve statements about behavior ("When I"), emotion ("I feel"), and impact ("because").

For example, the wife may say, "When I tell Mark that he can't eat anything before supper, and you permit him to do it, I feel angry and frustrated because it seems that I have no parental authority."

When this statement is made, the spouse is not to challenge it. Whether or not he thinks that he has countermanded your orders or that your parental authority is undercut by him, this *is* your view of things.

Here's where we get back to the need for a proper atmosphere for communication: There must be understanding and a desire to please. Without it, no communication of value will be possible. And if the husband refuses to understand your view of things, he is to be considered a saboteur. He need not agree with you. But with accurate empathy he must be able to see the situation through your eyes, not just his own.

*Feedback to the Statement of the Problem.* Next, you need feedback from him. Did he understand what you said in the statement of the problem? Can he repeat it back to you? And can he do this with an understanding attitude?

If he tells you what you said in a tone of voice or with an attitude that says, "You have no right to feel that way," you have failed to make adequate impact on him. If he does this, he will have sabotaged the communication, and again, it must be identified just that way: "sabotage!"

*Request for Change.* Once you are satisfied that he understands your point of view, you may make a request for change. Remember in chapter 8 I stated that "requesting" is one of the best ways to bring about change in a relationship.

In the illustration about Mark and his mother's concern, mother might frame her request this way: "What I would like is for you to respect the rules I lay down for Mark, and if you have a difference of opinion, talk with me privately about it." She is not asking that her word always be law but that they work together as a parental team and not undercut each other.

*Feedback to the Request for Change.* Again, feedback is necessary. Does the husband in this illustration understand what change she is asking for? If he understands what she is asking for, he should be able to repeat it. *This does not mean that he is agreeing to the request.* It does mean that he understands what she wants.

This is what I have called earlier "shared meaning." Before we can have agreement we must have understanding.

In this sequence it is totally inappropriate for the husband to criticize her request, demean it, or tell her that she has no right to make such a request. *Understanding* what change is desired is all important. Refusal to give adequate and accurate feedback is tantamount to sabotage and should be identified as such. It is not a matter of not being able to communicate. It is a matter of refusal to communicate; it is engaging in communication sabotage.

*Response.* Now it is the husband's turn. His wife wants to know, "How about it? Are you willing to do this?" She is making a request for response.

He must now decide what is in his interest. Can he make this change and still be true to himself and his own needs? He must be careful of several things at this point.

First, he must give himself time to think about the request for change. A quick "No" may indicate a spirit of ill-will and an unwillingness to do anything his wife wants. He may ask for time to think about it (see under next step).

Second, he must be careful not to derail his wife, by introducing a new issue. He may be tempted to say, "I don't think that we can even begin to settle this issue until we talk about your harsh attitude toward Mark."

It may be true that he's bothered by what he feels is her harsh attitude, but *let's take one thing at a time.* Let's get closure on this matter first, even if it is to turn down her request and set a date for the next engagement in which they will talk about "her harsh attitude." You cannot rush communication without running the risk of total confusion. One step at a time, please!

Third, be careful that you don't fall into bargaining—"If I go along with you on your request, then I expect you to go along with me on my thing." Remember that bargaining is foreign to the spirit of communication in a context of good-will. You do it because you care, not for what you are going to get out of it.

*Rejection or Acceptance.* The next step is rejection or acceptance. Having decided what he wants, the spouse may either reject the request for change or accept it conditionally or unconditionally. He may say, "I will do it under these conditions . . ." In the illustration of Mark, the husband may say, "I will go along with your directives to Mark so long as we can talk about my difference of opinion the same day."

With such a procedure it is entirely inappropriate to argue that the request for change is not wise, unreasonable —or even unscriptural! To do this is to sabotage the business at hand and get tied up in the unfruitful exercise of building a case as to why it should or should not be done. The issue is, "What changes do you need, and am I able to grant them and still be true to my own needs?" In a context of good-will, each is striving to understand and please the other. This offers the very best chance for success at communicating for change.

*Planning the Next Engagement and Closure.* Whatever the outcome of your attempt to communicate for change, new issues are not to be introduced at this point. It would only confuse the single issue you are attempting to communicate about. If another issue is to be considered, another engagement should be planned.

Another engagement should be planned anyway to make changes in the agreement you are presently formulating. No change should be cast in concrete but should be tentative until it stands the test of time.

The time of the next engagement will depend on how soon you want to get into new issues or how long you want to give the changes you have agreed on a chance to work. You may want to take up a new issue right away and continue on. But be careful you don't overload yourselves. At any rate, both the husband and wife should agree when this will be done. But remember, *don't put it off.*

After agreement on the change and the next engagement has been set there should be closure. That is to say, you both have agreed to a commitment to act, and that agreement is sealed by a physical expression of good-will, like a hug or kiss.

## OTHER CONSIDERATIONS IN COMMUNICATION FOR CHANGE

I asked Fay what observations she had about our methods of problem solving or communicating for change. She said half teasingly, "I didn't know we had any problems."

As I thought about that I realized that we really don't —at least no big unresolved conflicts hanging over our heads. And as we talked about it three things came into focus that we do in addition to the above.

*Keep Current.* We tend to keep current with each other's feelings. Every day we either check out each other or freely share our thoughts, feelings, and intentions. We know what our emotional temperature is each day, and if there are symptoms that something's wrong, we find out what it is.

*Don't Rush the Process.* When we are aware of what's wrong, we avoid rushing a solution. If you rush the process, you may not fully understand your own feelings or your spouse's feelings about the presenting problem. Not only that, if you take your time you may discover that the "presenting problem" is just a symptom of a deeper issue. Time will give you an opportunity to get a sharp focus on what's going on. Impatience is the enemy of good communication.

What is more, if you give yourself time to think about the problem, you will be able to get a sharper focus on the best possible change you can make. Fay and I are planning to move to our home on the Virginia section of the Chesapeake Bay in a few years where I want to pursue my writing ministry. With just the two of us there, I feel that we will have adequate room. Fay wants to put on an addition.

I have felt that the only reason she wants an addition is to have a place to put some of our expensive furniture from our Maryland home. So I have resisted it and suggested we sell the furniture.

We have plenty of time to decide what we'll finally do and have talked about it a lot. We have considered everything from various kinds of additions to none at all.

As I hear Fay talk now it sounds as though she wants the addition for more than a furniture showplace. She wants to do some entertaining. I'm willing now for a modest addition. But what we eventually do is not decided yet. The important thing is that we're open to hearing what each of us feels about the matter. We're giving ourselves time for those feelings to come into sharp focus.

*Emotional Imperative.* Finally, I notice that we tend to look for an "emotional imperative" in what each of us wants, particularly when each of us wants something different. For example, Fay may want "A," and I may want "B." But how badly does she need "A," and how badly do I need "B"? If on a scale of one to ten I'm a six and she's an eight, I instinctively concede to her because of the greater emotional imperative.

We have found by experience that two people in good mental health will strike a balance where, over the months, each will be yielding to the other about the same number of times. One caution must be exercised, however. Both must be totally aware of their feelings and the true emotional imperative, otherwise a false signal will be given.

### RATING YOUR COMMUNICATION FOR CHANGE

How well do you communicate for change? Here's a check list that may help you sort out what you do well and what you do poorly. Both the husband and wife should fill out a check list, and if a spirit of good-will prevails, they should compare their notes. They should avoid arguing over who is right and who is wrong. The purpose of comparing notes is to understand how each feels about their attempts to communicate for change.

Steps in communicating for change are listed in the check list with a description of what should have occurred (see left column) versus what should not have occurred (see right column). A "plus," "mid," or "minus" should be checked for each item. The wife may use one color pencil, and the husband another color. Or, each may make notes on separate sheets of paper.

"Plus" (+) means that you were successful in communicating that step.

"Mid" means that you were not totally successful.

"Minus" (−) means that you were not successful in achieving the goal for that step.

If you are not able to get through all the steps, draw a line under the last step you completed and make a brief statement as to why you got no further. Was it communication sabotage? Lack of time? What?

See check list beginning on next page.

### Engagement

The engagement was requested with a clear request for communication about a specific issue. It was accepted or postponed to a specific time, which was later honored.

*vs.*

The request for an engagement was not clear. There was talk about communication but not a specific request for an engagement. The issue was not specific. It was postponed and the postponement was not honored or rejected.

(+)＿＿ (Mid) ＿＿ (−) ＿＿

### Statement of Your Problem

The problem was stated as an "I" message or in a non-attacking way. It was specific. The problem was not challenged by the other spouse as invalid. The listener seemed eager to hear what the problem was.

*vs.*

The problem was stated in an attacking way. It was vague. It was challenged by the other spouse as invalid. The listener did not seem eager to hear what the speaker had to say and gave verbal and non-verbal messages to that effect.

(+) ＿＿ (Mid) ＿＿ (−) ＿＿

### Request for Change

The request for change was specific. It was received willingly. There was no verbal or non-verbal message that would discourage the speaker from making a request for change.

*vs.*

The request was not specific. It was not received willingly. This was seen in the rejection of the messages.

(+) ＿＿ (Mid) ＿＿ (−) ＿＿

*Feedback to the Request for Change*

The spouse who received the request was able to restate the request with a respectful, non-challenging attitude. *vs.* The spouse could not restate the request for change, or if he did, he gave the message that the speaker had no right to ask for such a change.

$$(+) \underline{\hspace{1cm}} (\text{Mid}) \underline{\hspace{1cm}} (-) \underline{\hspace{1cm}}$$

*Response*

The recipient of the request gave himself time to think about it, did not try to derail, and avoided bargaining. The response was made in a respectful and hopeful manner. *vs.* The respondent continued to give verbal or non-verbal messages that the request was unreasonable or that he was refusing to respond because of the unreasonableness of the request. He was quick to say "No," he tried to derail, or he attempted to bargain.

$$(+) \underline{\hspace{1cm}} (\text{Mid}) \underline{\hspace{1cm}} (-) \underline{\hspace{1cm}}$$

*Rejection or Acceptance*

There was a clear acceptance of the proposed change (conditionally or unconditionally), or a rejection. Any conditions made were clear. There was no attempt to avoid accepting or rejecting the change by getting into an argument over what was requested. *vs.* The proposed change was neither accepted nor rejected; that decision was avoided. If it was accepted with condition, the conditions were not clear.

$$(+) \underline{\hspace{1cm}} (\text{Mid}) \underline{\hspace{1cm}} (-) \underline{\hspace{1cm}}$$

*Planning the Next Engagement and Closure*

*vs.*

Refusal to set a time for a new engagement and refusal to give closure with a physical expression of good-will.

If agreement was reached, a time was set to reexamine it for purposes of making any further changes. If no agreement was reached, a new engagement was set to talk about the most important issue yet unresolved. Closure was declared with a physical expression of good-will.

(+) _____ (Mid) _____ (−) _____

*Summary.* Change that comes about through effective communication is not a "horse trade." It is a unilateral decision made in an atmosphere where there is a respect of differentness and a thorough understanding of the changes desired, and where there is a desire to change to please self and spouse.

The methodology given in this chapter is only a learning aid. Couples who communicate in a context of good-will soon learn to employ its principles as a natural part of communication for change.

# Beware of Crazymakers

—BY ANDRÉ

IF YOU FAITHFULLY PRACTICE the principles of communication outlined in the foregoing chapters, you will improve your communication style. But I must warn you that with some people, in spite of your best efforts at communicating, you will fail miserably.

In this chapter and the next we need to look at reasons why you won't always be able to communicate. It takes two to communicate. If your spouse really doesn't want to communicate, then your attempts will be thwarted—though I do make some suggestions as to what might be done.

In this chapter we'll see how crazymakers thwart communication. In the next chapter we'll consider manipulators and other "non-communicators."

## WHAT IS A CRAZYMAKER?

It is naïve to suppose that everyone wants to communicate effectively—to understand and be understood. Some people are afraid of understanding and being understood simply because they may have to examine their differences honestly and openly. Many people simply don't want to do that. They want their own way. Any communication that threatens to keep them from having their way, or will force them to change, they will sabotage.

This, in short, is what a crazymaker is. He is a communication saboteur. "Crazymaking" is a term coined by George Bach and Yetta Bernhard in their book *Aggression Lab*. They define it as "a subtle yet persistent strategy of one person or a group to upset the composure or psychological equilibrium ('having your head together') of another individual or group of individuals"[1]

Crazymakers actually sabotage communication by upsetting the composure of those who would try to communicate. The victim of crazymaking leaves the scene with his mind in confusion, actually feeling as if he's going crazy.

Crazymaking cannot be accomplished, however, without a willing victim.

Take, for example, the wife who wants to talk about a problem, but whenever she does, her husband explodes. His explosiveness is a crazymaker known as "short fuse." He sabotages communication by making her afraid to bring up subjects he doesn't want to talk about.

If she tries to talk to him about his short fuse, he will blow up about that too. So to avoid the blowup, she avoids talking about anything that disturbs him. She then becomes the willing victim of crazymaking. He sabotages communication by threatening to blow up. She obliges by not saying anything that will cause him to blow up.

"Crazymaking," according to Bach and Bernhard, "is the most subtle and camouflaged of the many forms of *passive-aggressive hostility.*"[2] The behavior is "aggressive" because it pushes for one's own way. But it is "passive" in that it pushes in a covert and sneaky way. The passive-aggressive crazymaker needs to mask his intentions in order to be an effective saboteur.

## METHODS OF CRAZYMAKING

Various methods of crazymaking are used.[3] But all of them have the effect of upsetting the victim's composure. Here are fourteen of the more popular methods.

*Violation of Context.* Every conversation takes place in a context. The communicators have an understanding about the purpose of their discussion and the rules they will follow. For example, the wife who approaches her husband with an "I" message is saying by this approach that she wants to talk about a problem in a context of good-will. In this context, attack and defense are inappropriate. It also means that she is seeking understanding, not agreement.

Her husband may not want to talk about the problem. Indeed, if understanding is generated, he may be put in the position of having to change. To keep this from happening he may accuse her of attacking him. He may become very defensive of his behavior. What began as a context of good-will turns out, by the husband's decision, to be a context of ill-will.

Even though the wife proceeds slowly and carefully, the husband may at any time violate the context and tell her that she is attacking him. When that happens, she must be careful not to defend herself, which will play into his hands. Defense means that it is a context of ill-will. Instead, she must address the issue of crazymaking.

She must say, "Honey, I think we have a crazymaking problem here. The context is being violated. I'm really trying hard to communicate in a context of good-will and be non-attacking and non-defensive. But no matter how hard I try, I'm told that I'm attacking, and I get defensive replies."

This may not make the husband stop crazymaking. But it will address the real issue. Their inability to communicate is *not* due to ill-will on the wife's part. It is due to the husband's communication sabotage. Every time he hears something he doesn't like, he simply declares that he is being attacked. The solution to this couple's problem must begin with the husband's willingness not to sabotage the process.

*Switch of Assumptions.* A variation of "violation of context" is "switch of assumptions." This occurs when we think we have agreed on what our problem is, but the crazymaker switches that assumption to something different.

Harry and Melba sought marriage counseling because of Harry's infidelity. It had shattered Melba's trust in him. As we got into the problem of the infidelity and the difficulty of rebuilding trust, Harry grew more and more uncomfortable. One day without warning he declared in the counseling session, "It's true that I was guilty of infidelity, but that's not our real problem. Our real problem is Melba's spending habits." He then proceeded to launch into a lengthy complaint about the way she handled money.

It was true that they had money problems. But in no way was it related to the damage created by the infidelity, and it was definitely a minor problem. By switching assumptions, however, Harry was trying to get away from a painful issue that he really didn't want to discuss.

I refused to get into a debate over which issue was more important. If I did, I would have fallen victim to the "derailing" crazymaker. I simply pointed out that switching assumptions would keep us from the real issue that had brought them in—infidelity and the shattering of trust. And if Harry insisted on switching assumptions, I could only assume that he was trying to crazymake to keep from discussing the more painful issue of infidelity and trust.

*The Double Bind.* This style of crazymaking is similar to the previous two. It differs slightly, however. Here the victim is put in the place where he is wrong if he does and wrong if he doesn't.

Take the case of Lori and Jay. They continually fought over his erratic time of arrival home from work. They finally agreed that if he was going to be late he was to call her. But when Jay called, Lori would attack him as an inconsiderate person for not coming home "on time." The net result was that Jay was wrong if he did call, and wrong if he didn't call.

In this case Lori was not permitting communication to take place. She was sabotaging it by making her husband wrong whichever way he went.

Why should she want to do this? Lori simply didn't like her husband. She wanted to demonstrate that it was hopelessly impossible to communicate and that their marriage was beyond repair. She really wanted to get out of the marriage, but couldn't admit it to Jay or to herself. The issue was not the way Jay handled his erratic schedule. The issue was a double bind, which Lori used to punish her husband and demonstrate that their marriage couldn't be saved.

*The Set Up.* This one is used when the crazymaker doesn't want to do something but wants to avoid the responsibility of having to say no. Suppose a man wants to have sexual relations with his wife, but she won't say "No" because she doesn't want to take the responsibility for being unresponsive. She will do something she knows will provoke him, like paying the newspaper boy out of his coin collection. He blows up and is ugly about it. Then she goes for the kill and says that she couldn't possibly be sexually responsive to such an ugly man.

She has accomplished her objective. She doesn't have to have sex, *or* take the blame for refusing her husband. She sets him up to do it for her.

Alcoholics are great at the set up. They make it a habit to blame their drinking on other people, particularly wife and children. The argument goes, "You'd drink, too, if you were married to the woman I'm married to." If the normal problems in living with his wife don't provide the alcoholic with a reason to excuse his drinking, he'll set her up. He will do or say something outrageous, and when his wife blows up, he has an excuse to retreat to his bottle.

To argue over the coin collection, or whatever the alcoholic may use for the set up, is to miss the real issue. The real issue is the crazymaker known as the "set up." In the example of the coin collection, the husband needs to say in a non-attacking way, "I feel as if I've been set up," and then address the issue of crazymaking rather than the coin collection. This is a form of metacommunication. He is attempting to address what went wrong with the communication process.

In dealing with the alcoholic, spouse and children must be aware of the set up and not feel guilty for another drunken episode. I know families that are in constant agony because they try so hard not to drive the alcoholic to drink. They are not driving anyone to drink. Drinking is the alcoholic's responsibility, not the family's.

*Reality Denial.* Every person has his own perception of reality. Let's say the husband reveals his perception of reality, and the wife insists that the perception is not correct. The effect is to throw the husband off balance psychologically. It may even make him doubt his ability to be accurate concerning his interpretation of anything. The crazymaker is then able to substitute his own interpretation of reality.

The facts about any matter may be argued. But that person's perception of reality and how he feels about it cannot be argued. He knows how he sees the issue. He feels about it more strongly than anyone else, whether or not that perspective or those feelings may be justified.

Donna is a good case in point. She told me that she was becoming cold and indifferent toward Jake, her husband, for some unexplained reason. She couldn't understand why.

She then unfolded an incredible story. Jake would not work because he couldn't find a job he liked, or the people at work didn't treat him right. He just sat at home watching TV or went out drinking with his buddies.

He expected Donna to keep up with their two children, keep house, and work, since he "couldn't find a decent job."

They had no washer or dryer so she had to wash her clothes at the laundromat. Since he insisted that baby sitting was "woman's work," she had to take the children with her.

Jake made his version of reality so persuasive that Donna couldn't see what he was doing to her. She couldn't see that Jake's demands were totally unrealistic and that he was failing to carry his weight in the marriage. She was convinced that his view was correct and hers was wrong.

Because Donna was a willing victim of crazymaking, she couldn't understand what was going wrong with the marriage. Only when she began to get a grip on reality did she put Jake in the position of having to mend his ways. She confronted Jake. She told him that she felt she was the victim of crazymaking (which she explained to him). His crazymaker was "reality denial." She wasn't going to play the game any more. She no longer would accept his version of reality, and if he didn't carry some of the family responsibility, the work simply wouldn't be done.

A variation of "reality denial" is the crazymaker's attempt to make the victim feel guilty or ashamed of his perception of reality. He will say, "You mean you *really* feel that way?" with the implication, "How could you?"

Jake tried to pull this with me when I talked with him. Because Donna was on the verge of a nervous breakdown, I suggested that she spend the weekend away from home to get herself together. Jake called me and said, "I can't believe that you told my wife to stay away this weekend. What kind of counselor are you?"

I pointed out that he was doing to me exactly what he was doing to Donna. He tried to make me feel guilty for my perception of reality, so that I would not act on it. He did this three times in less than a minute. His pitch was that good counseling gets families together; it doesn't break them apart. I refused to play the game, but instead pointed out that if his version of reality was the only one, then we had nothing further to discuss.

*Derailing.* This crazymaker breaks the victim's line of reasoning by switching to a different issue. He will change the subject or distract the victim to break his concentration.

Dave is an example. Even though he had come for counseling with his wife, Della, he didn't want to talk about his feelings. Della freely talked about hers. When I asked Dave to share his feelings about what Della was saying, he talked about *her* feelings. He was attempting to derail me here by talking about her feelings rather than his own.

When I pointed out that he was not talking about his own feelings, but Della's, he attempted to tie me up in a discussion about Della's feelings. When that didn't work, he attempted to derail me by moving to a more abstract subject—whether or not people really ought to talk about their feelings, complete with illustrations of the bad things that come from talking about feelings.

I pointed out to Dave that he was derailing me. The subject at hand was *his feelings.* This was one of the few times that a crazymaker admitted to me that he was crazymaking. Tearfully, he said that he didn't want to talk about his feelings. Too much was bottled up, and he was afraid of what would happen if he let loose.

*Blamesmanship.* This crazymaker blames the victim for disrupting communication. It usually starts with the crazymaker's doing something inappropriate. When the victim reacts negatively, the crazymaker reacts as though he has been attacked unjustly. He defends his behavior as "just a little thing." Or he says that he didn't know he would be "misinterpreted," or that it would be "taken so hard." The crazymaker's refusal to accept blame usually makes the victim step up his blaming attack. Then he seems to be the one who is creating the disorder. This crazymaker is similar to the "set up."

*Bugging.* Anyone who has children knows how they can bug each other. Mimicking, making faces, pushing, grabbing the last cookie on the plate are all childish ways of bugging. But adults bug too.

George and Rachael had only one car. He usually commuted to work in it two days a week. Rachael didn't need the car very often, but occasionally she liked to get out of the house and go to a shopping mall to walk around. Almost without exception, whenever she wanted the car, George "needed" it for some reason. Rachael was generally an even-tempered person. But whenever George would do this, she became furious.

Why did George do this? He was not a happy person, and it annoyed him that Rachael could communicate so calmly and reasonably. He was annoyed that nothing seemed to bother her. The car was one thing he could use to bug her.

He delighted in seeing how many things he could bug her about. In his thinking he was "cutting her down to size." But in the process, he was making havoc of all her attempts to communicate calmly and reasonably. George felt at a disadvantage in communicating with Rachael. By bugging her, he kept her from communicating calmly and reasonably. And when they couldn't communicate, he was able to do whatever he wanted to do simply "because they couldn't talk about their differences."

*Overloading.* Crazymakers use at least two overloading techniques. One is "command overload." This happens when demands for change come too fast.

Norman declared to me that his marriage was beyond repair. Too many things were wrong. His wife, Betty, believed that they could solve their problems if they took them one at a time.

My intuition told me that Norman really didn't want to communicate. Estranged from Betty, he was going his own way, and he seemed to like that. Now this was being threatened by Betty, who was looking for a solution to the estrangement.

After several counseling sessions, Norman became agitated and said, "All right, then, if you want to save this marriage, here are some changes that need to be made." He poured out a torrent of demands that could not possibly be filled all at once.

When I pointed this out he gave me a triumphant, "Ah hah! Didn't I tell you this marriage couldn't be saved?"

Again, I wouldn't play the game. I pointed out that he was crazymaking with "command overload." We could solve the problems one at a time if he were willing. Was he willing or was he going to continue to crazymake? The ball was back in his court. Unfortunately, Norman tried to play his game to the bitter end. Betty's only consolation was that she understood it was Norman's crazymaking, not her inability to solve their problems, that kept them from saving the marriage.

Another crazymaking overload is "volume overload." The crazymaker uses more words and ideas than the victim can possibly process. The non-verbal person will find his mind boggled with verbiage and will not be able to think clearly. The crazymaker will then declare that the situation is hopeless and quite beyond solution. They "just can't seem to discuss the problem."

The victim, feeling incapable of sorting out the issues, may be tempted to agree and lapse into despair—unless he recognizes that the crazymaker has sabotaged the communication by overloading him with too many words or ideas. Again, the prime defense is to identify the problem for what it is—*crazymaking*, this time by overload.

*The Double Whammy.* This is constant, intensive attention —like a fixed gaze that emotionally overwhelms the victim. It so rattles him that he can't get his ideas together. Sometimes the look is a threatening one that seems to say, "If you say anything out of the way, you'll be sorry." Dominant husbands use this effectively with submissive wives.

Sometimes the look is disdainful. John was such a person.

He almost succeeded in using this on me. He had agreed to counseling only after much pleading by his wife.

He had impressive credentials and socialized with the "greats" around Washington. I found this intimidating enough. But what made matters worse, when he talked to me, he looked as if he were smelling something bad.

I was having a difficult time getting anywhere because I felt intimidated. Finally I realized that he was using his double whammy to sabotage communication. I called this to his attention and said, "Do you smell something bad?" He looked surprised and said, "No." I said, "Whenever you look at me, you curl your lip and distend your nostrils. When you talk I feel as if I'm dirt. I get the distinct impression that you find it distasteful to talk to me." He denied that this was so, but he couldn't keep up the double whammy without my calling his attention to it. After awhile he stopped doing it, and we began to get somewhere.

*Moving the Beltline* Most people have an emotional beltline that is easily located. You know what subjects are "below the beltline" and what subjects are safe. Whenever this crazymaker gets in a tight place and doesn't want to talk about the problem, he claims that you're hitting below the belt. Since you never know where his beltline is, you are forced to play it safe and keep the conversation superficial.

Carol used this effectively whenever her husband tried to talk about her mother's interference in their lives. Sometimes it was okay for Fred to talk about her mother. Other times Carol would break off the discussion with, "I will not permit you to talk about my mother." Fred never did know when it was and was not safe to talk about mother. My attempts to get Carol to talk about this beltline was difficult. She didn't want to say what statements about mother were above the beltline and what were below. If she established a beltline on the subject, she couldn't keep moving it and cutting off discussion about mother.

Again, I had to call it what it was—crazymaking, and until she quit the crazymaking we couldn't get on with a solution.

*The Stickler.* This is used by the crazymaker who, having learned some of the rules of communication, bogs down the process by sticking to the letter of each law and arguing about the rules.

Pete, for example, was guilty of derailing. I caught him at it so many times that he had to admit it and quit it. But then he switched to "the stickler." Every time his wife or I introduced a new topic into the conversation he accused us of derailing. We had changed the subject. A lengthy conversation followed about the rules. By using the "stickler," he managed to tie us up in long discussions about the rules of communication rather than the problem at hand. With imaginative genius he managed to use "the stickler" to derail us once again!

Why does a person do something like this? The answer is that he really doesn't want to understand or be understood. If effective communication takes place, he may have to mend his ways! So he sabotages it.

*Being Flip.* This is used by the crazymaker who is the opposite of the stickler. He really doesn't take the rules of communication seriously. Or if he does go along with them, he has a condescending attitude. Or he makes fun of the rules. He often laughs a great deal or approaches communication with mock sincerity. He gives you the impression that he just is not taking the whole thing seriously.

The flip attitude of this crazymaker is the issue that must be addressed. You must say, "I find it difficult to communicate because I get the impression that you're not taking this matter seriously." If he claims that he is, you might ask him if it's all right for you to point out every time he is flip, and if he would stop being flip when you point it out to him.

You may find it difficult getting that kind of agreement, however. The incorrigible crazymaker will continue it. Then you must identify the problem for what it is—crazymaking by being flip. Communication cannot take place when a saboteur is at work.

*The Short Fuse.* I used this as an illustration of crazymaking at the beginning of the chapter. The "short fuse" is that crazymaker who lets you know verbally and non-verbally that he is unhappy and likely to blow up at any moment. This makes the victim proceed carefully so as not to do anything to make "short fuse" blow up.

Sometimes "short fuse" uses the "set up." He will provoke the victim to say something that may hurt or offend him, and then he will blow up when it happens.

## HOW TO FIGHT CRAZYMAKERS

Crazymakers are sneaky. Their hostility is always camouflaged so they need not take the blame for any communication disaster. Even the "short fuse," though he blows up, takes the approach, "You *knew* that would make me blow up. *You* are responsible for the explosion." This tactic is designed to make you even more careful about not doing anything to make him blow up.

The best way to stop crazymaking is to confront it. When you recognize the pattern, stop and say, "You're crazymaking me!" Then, if you're permitted, describe to the crazymaker what is happening to you.

Having been called on his game of crazymaking, the super-crazymaker will reach into his bag of tricks and use a different one. You must be willing to call him on every one of his tricks. Only when crazymaking is exposed does it become ineffective.

This is why a naïve and unbiblical view of the wife's submission must be corrected if there is to be good communication. When communication sabotage is taking place and the husband is guilty of it, the wife must be able to call it to his attention.

The super-crazymaker, seeing his games destroyed, will most likely try to keep you from talking about his crazymaking. The double bind is often used. Or, he may even declare that talking about his crazymaking is hitting below the belt!

Bach and Bernhard offer some advice for dealing with crazymakers:

> Remember . . . that crazymakers prefer to express their hostilities toward their S.O. [significant other] in passive-aggressive rather than impact-aggressive ways. One way, therefore, to fight a crazymaker is—to use a hunter's term—to flush him out: locate the crazymaking behavior pattern and "shoot." CONFRONT! Shout STOP IT, loud and clear. Call it what it is—not simply "foul," but CRAZYMAKING! The constructive fighting strategy here is based on the belief that crazymakers prefer that their destructive manipulations do not show. They prefer camouflaged hostility to a leveling style of displaying anger. They wish to hurt, weaken, or embarrass you, but they do not like being caught in the act. So your basic countermove is always, "Call it!" And let your embarrassment, instead of hindering you, be your guide. Do not allow yourself to avoid confrontation out of shame at being trapped in a crazymaker. Do not display false pride, just admit: "OK, you got me this time. Just be sure it doesn't happen again."[4]

Some of that may sound a bit strong for the woman who is just learning that assertiveness is not unbiblical. But don't miss the spirit of what they're saying. Remember, if you conspire to let the crazymaking go by without identifying it as such, you are just as guilty as the crazymaker for communication failure.

Another way to break crazymaking patterns is in communication workshops in which the group can bring to bear its collective observations. Private counsel is also helpful. A skillful counselor usually can spot crazymaking. I say "usually" because even the best counselors are beaten by the crazymaker from time to time. I had such an experience early in my counseling practice.

One of my clients was a man who is an absolute tyrant. He tyranized his wife at home, and in my office he would intimidate and crazymake me by alternating between the Short Fuse and withdrawal or Overload and withdrawal. He and his wife had been in counseling several months, and I was helping them communicate for change. He was really feeling the pressure to make changes he didn't want to make.

One week they came in and the wife, who prior to this looked like a washed-out rag, was positively radiant. He was quiet. She felt that they had a good week, even though she hadn't honored the change they had agreed on the previous week. In fact, the day after they agreed to the change, she told him that it couldn't possibly work, so he agreed to drop it and make no demands on her at all.

Having freedom from her tyrannical husband's demands, she came alive and stopped fighting with him. Even he had to admit that it was a good week. But then came the crazymaker. He shouted at me, "Last week we made an agreement. I paid good money to get my wife into counseling, and she made an agreement that she broke the next day!"

By this time I was tired of his intimidation and complaints about my fee. I asked him if he wanted to drop out of counseling. He said he did and that was that.

Later I realized what he had done. First he used the Stickler—she had broken the contract, and that was against the rules. It didn't matter that the week was the best one they had had in years. He was going to stick to the rules. Second, he set me up with a complaint about having paid me for a wasted session. He counted on my reacting to his complaint, and I did. He set me up because he saw that I was effectively challenging his game of tyranny. He got out from under the pressure to change by crazymaking.

# 15

# Manipulators and Other Non-Communicators

## —By André

IN THE LAST CHAPTER we looked at communication saboteurs called "crazymakers." In this chapter I want to develop further the caution I raised in the last chapter. Don't suppose that you will be able to communicate with everyone. Not only do crazymakers block good communications, manipulators and other "non-communicators" will do it too.

It's not really accurate to talk about "non-communicators" because, as we will see, you cannot *not* communicate. I call them "non-communicators" to distinguish them from crazymakers, who are communication saboteurs. Manipulators and other "non-communicators" I describe don't set out to sabotage communication. Their defenses keep them from communicating effectively.

### UNDERSTANDING THE MANIPULATOR

My book *You Can Change Your Personality* was written in part to help people understand the unbalanced behavior inside us that attempts to find self-worth and hold down anxiety by controlling others. The manipulator cannot communicate effectively because he feels that he will be at a disadvantage if he asks for what he wants honestly and openly. So he goes about getting what he wants by the devious means of controlling people.

Psychologist Everett L. Shostrom has written an excellent book on this subject called *Man, the Manipulator*. [1] He says several important things that should help us identify the manipulator.

The manipulator disguises his true feelings. He thinks that if he reveals them, people will catch on to what he's up to. If they do that, they may not do what he wants them to do, whether it's do his laundry or be his friend. He also tends to treat people as things—objects to be used, rather than creatures with feelings. He may wear a façade that pretends caring. But the genuine person can spot it as phony.

He tends to blame others for his failures. He refuses to take responsibility, except in a sick way where he makes himself responsible for everything. But that too is manipulative, because he gets others to take these burdens off his back by moaning about how heavy they are.

## MANIPULATIVE TYPES

Let's look at the manipulative types for a more precise understanding. I am using the categories that Shostrom uses. In parentheses are the categories I use in *You Can Change Your Personality*.

*The Dictator* (The Autocratic Personality). This manipulator emphasizes strength. Here are some of his behaviors: domination of others, acting impressed with his own importance, planning the lives of other people for them, acting dictatorial, insisting his way is best, expecting others to obey and admire him, always engaging in some activity to show off his physical or intellectual ability, justifying his behavior, and being excessively planful. [2]

His target is usually the weakling who finds it difficult to resist forceful people. The Dictator does not need to ask for what he wants. Since he is "king," he simply leans on the weak, who do obeisance to him. Communication between equals is impossible because the Dictator has no equal.

*The Weakling* (The Self-Effacing Personality). The Weakling has ways of dealing with the Dictator that are just as manipulative and sneaky as the Dictator's ways. He forgets, doesn't hear, or is passively silent.

He may even conquer the Dictator by being so weak he has to be hospitalized or put in a mental institution where the Dictator has to take care of him.

He does not communicate as an equal either. If he did, his wishes might be denied. But because he is so "helpless" and "weak," no "decent human being" could deny such a needy person. He gets what he wants by being weak rather than by asking. Wives of dictatorial husbands often out-maneuver their husbands with this manipulation.

Some of the weakling's behaviors are extreme manifestations of weakness, lack of verbal and physical assertiveness, self-depreciation, extreme self-criticism, continual rumination over right and wrong, acceptance of depression as an excuse for immobility, and giving in too easily.[3]

*The Calculator* (The Exploitive Personality). The Calculator attempts to control other people. He differs from the Dictator in that he is more hostile. Here are some of his typical behaviors: exhibitionism and self-enhancement, always talking about himself and building himself up, defensiveness and self-justification, superior attitudes, intense concern over grooming and dress, independent to the degree he feels he needs no one, ruthless, always needing to win in competition, seductiveness and flirtatiousness, compulsively seeking success, and self-righteousness.[4]

As with the Dictator, the Calculator doesn't ask for what

he wants. He cons people. He does not communicate as an equal with others because he is independent of all. If he needs, he either cons or takes it by fierce competition.

*The Clinging Vine* (The Dependent Personality). The Clinging Vine does the opposite of the Calculator. He (though more often it is "she") emphasizes his dependency and as such is the natural target for the Calculator. But he has his way of getting what he wants too. He pretends to be totally helpless and gets what he wants by baiting the Calculator's need to control. The Calculator sees him as a pushover and takes control. The Clinging Vine doesn't ask for what he wants as an equal among equals either. He, as the Weakling, needs to be helpless to get his way. If he became equal, people might not see him as such a needy person and might say, "No." So he gets what he wants without asking.

The Clinging Vine differs from the Weakling in that he tends to be a little more affectionate. Here are some of his typical behaviors: extreme dependency, letting others take care of his needs, unwillingness to make decisions, unwillingness to talk back, believing anyone, behaving like a parasite, and acting like a perpetual child.[5]

*The Bully* (The Aggressive Personality). This is the tough guy who threatens and intimidates. He doesn't ask for what he wants. He scares it out of you.

The Nice Guy is his usual target because the Nice Guy always wants to please and can't stand hostility. The Bully differs from the Dictator and Calculator in that he is the most hostile of the three. Here are some of his behaviors: insensitive, cruel, harsh and judgmental, self-righteousness, verbally and/or physically attacking, hostile, verbally and/or physically abusive, quarrelsome, and excessively strict and rigid.[6]

*The Nice Guy* (The Overconventional Personality). The Nice Guy is the opposite of the Bully. He exaggerates love, affection, and caring. He gets what he wants, not by asking, but by being so nice that people feel guilty if they don't do what he wants. He never asks for what he wants, but he can act terribly hurt if he doesn't get it.

He's harder to cope with than the Bully. It's much easier to say "No" to a bully. Here are some typical behaviors of the Nice Guy: smiling continually, agreeing with everyone, overly eager to please, not expressing negative feelings, letting others have their way all the time, liking and accepting everyone without discrimination.[7]

*The Judge* (The Distrustful Personality). Distrust is the primary behavior of the Judge. He, as the other manipulators, gets what he wants, not by asking, but by controlling people in his own unique way. He continually puts others in the position of having to prove or vindicate themselves. By so doing, they wind up giving the Judge what he wants as a way to get back into his favor. His most frequent target is the Protector, who needs to show his helpfulness and good-will. Here are some of his typical behaviors: extreme cynicism, constant fault-finding, jealousy, unforgiving spirit, and never believing anything that's said.[8]

*The Protector* (The Hypernormal Personality). This personality is the opposite of the Judge. He cares for and helps others. He is the "Unselfish One" and "Martyr." He is similar to the Nice Guy, but more dominant and protective. But, like the Nice Guy, he gets his way by being kind and helpful. How could you deny someone who is so unselfish? He does not need to ask. He simply expects people to "do right" by him, since he is such a giving person, and he knows how to make people feel guilty when they don't.

The Judge, however, usually wins in a contest with the Protector. The Protector always has to prove that the Judge's cynicism is unwarranted, but the Judge usually remains unmoved. This is generally true of passive-aggressive behavior.

This person tends to triumph over the active personality because he need do nothing to win. Here are some of the Protector's behaviors: overgenerous, too kind to others, always sympathetic to everyone, too easy going, too accepting, and spoils others with kindness.[9]

*Summary.* In every case the manipulator tries to control people with his behavior. He does not trust other people to give him what he needs, so he is dishonest about his needs.

Some manipulators *actively* try to dominate the weak to get what they want. Sometimes they *passively* play stupid and "underdog" to pull what they want from the unsuspecting "top dogs." Some extract what they want by *threat*—they make people afraid of them. Finally, some pull what they want from others by making them *feel guilty.* But typical of all is getting what they want by control rather than by asking for it honestly and openly, which would reveal their thoughts, feelings, and intentions.

## OTHER NON-COMMUNICATORS

There are certain axioms or self-evident truths about communication that help us understand four other types of people who are impossible to communicate with. These all violate one of these axioms.

*The "Non-Communicator."* It's not technically correct to call someone a "non-communicator." There is no such thing as "non-communication." But I use this label to point out that type of communicator who tries to violate one of the axioms of communication, which is this: "You cannot *not* communicate."[10] Communication involves both words *and behavior.* A person may not say a thing, *but he cannot not behave.* Indeed, if he is behaving as though he does not want to communicate, you get a very definite message, which is a communication. The fellow-passenger on an airplane who sits with his eyes closed is giving you the message that he doesn't want to talk.

Because he is a stranger, no offense is taken. That stranger has made no commitment to you. Therefore if he wants to convey a behavioral message that says he doesn't want to talk, that's his privilege.

In marriage, however, that "message" is an offense. Marriage involves commitment of two people to each other. When the "non-communicator" gives such a behavioral message, he raises a serious question about that commitment. By acting as though he doesn't want to talk, *he acts as though no commitment exists*—much like the stranger on the airplane.

But the "non-communicator" in marriage tends to go one step further. When he is asked, "Why don't you want to talk to me?" he acts surprised, claims innocence and denies that he doesn't want to talk. He may even go so far as to say, "I never said I didn't want to talk to you."

Whatever his defense, he will deny that his behavior is communicating the very definite message, "I don't want to talk to you." Or, if he does admit that he's "not very talkative," he will treat it as benign behavior and act as though you're getting all worked up over nothing. Such a response leads to a dead-end and to frustration.

"Non-communicators" have developed the philosophy over the years that they are safe when they are silent and when they don't let people into their inner world. But they do not understand or take seriously the fact that their silence conveys an important message about the relationship. It is saying, "I want to keep you out of my inner world." Their silence implies by that message: "I have no commitment to let you get close to me."

The spouse who experiences this kind of estrangement cannot let the "non-communicator" escape responsibility for this message. He must be charged with breaking a commitment to closeness and be expected to mend his ways. Implicit in marriage is a commitment to closeness, which involves touching each other in the inner world of thoughts, feelings, and intentions.

*The "Relationship" Non-Communicator.* This non-communicator takes responsibility only for the content of what he says and not for what his message implies about the relationship. He will not address the issue of the relationship.

For example, he may say to his wife, "If you never check the oil in the car you'll ruin the engine in no time." There are two messages here. The first message deals with *content:* "It's imperative to check the oil in the car regularly." The second message deals with their *relationship:* "I am angry at your carelessness over letting the oil level get low." Now if the wife says, "Are you angry with me?" he will say, "Whatever gave you that idea? All I said was, 'If you never check the oil in the car you'll ruin the engine in no time.'" He denies that this message says anything about their relationship or his attitude toward the relationship.

The "relationship non-communicator" must be charged with the responsibility of communicating *both* a content and a relationship message.

His wife may say, "If you had said, 'Honey, please be sure to check the oil in the car every time you get gas,' I would have gotten a more friendly message."

The incorrigible non-communicator will probably reply, "You're imagining things, and you're too sensitive." But in reality he is denying one of the axioms of communication, which says that every communication has both a content and a relationship aspect.[11] That is, the message not only has content, but it is also a commentary on the relationship.

The wife in this illustration might say to her husband, "Tell me how you feel about our relationship." If he refuses to talk about it, he will be telling something about the relationship. If he claims that the relationship is fine, but his behavior and messages say otherwise, you're dealing with "incongruence" (see page 83).

Even though your communication may not get any better, at least you know what's wrong!

*The "I Do Because You Do" Non-Communicator.* This is a type of "non-communication" in that each spouse keeps communication from taking place. Suppose a couple has a marital problem and the husband blames it on his wife's nagging. He says she nags, so he reacts by withdrawing. But she says that's not the way it is. The problem is his withdrawal. He withdraws so she nags.

He sees the sequence of events this way: nagging and withdrawal, nagging and withdrawal *(ad infinitum)*. She sees the sequence of events this way: withdrawal and nagging, withdrawal and nagging *(ad infinitum)*.[12] Each is saying, "I do what I do because you do what you do." Neither takes responsibility for initiating the action, and therefore neither takes responsibility for stopping! The best way to intervene is to get each to take the responsibility for his own behavior. She does not have to respond to his withdrawal by nagging. He does not have to respond to her nagging by withdrawing.

*The "I Never Said That" Non-Communicator.* People not only communicate words, but they communicate words in a particular way. The manner in which we speak tells the listener something about the relationship. No matter what the words say, the manner carries an entirely separate message.

For example, a dog does not understand the words his owner uses. But he does understand a friendly and unfriendly manner. The owner may say to the dog in a harsh tone, with a frown on his face, "You're the most wonderful friend I have. I love you." But the dog will put his tail between his legs and cower in the corner. The master's way of expressing himself carries a message all of its own.

Likewise, the master may say in loving tones, "I'm going to grind you into hamburger and feed you to the neighbor's cat," and the dog will wag his tail and lick his master's hand. Again, the master's way of expressing himself carries a message all its own.

The "I never said that" non-communicator denies that

his manner colors his message. Or, he will deny that his manner communicates what the listener interpreted it to mean. Like the "relationship non-communicator," he refuses to take responsibility for the relationship part of the message. He must be charged with that responsibility if there is to be any hope at better communication.

*Summary.* Manipulators and other non-communicators must be handled like the crazymaker. Their tactics must be exposed for what they are, and you must call *foul!* In a context of good-will, the manipulator or non-communicator may be willing to learn. And you as an informed person are his best chance for help. No one else knows why communication seems to be hopeless, but *you* do. It is not hopeless! A saboteur is at work, and he needs to be stopped. Muster your skills and get to work on him. Every communication saboteur that is stopped means stronger homes and stronger marriages.

# Checklist of Communication Principles

To help you think through the book and remember the principles of communication you have read, here's a convenient check list. When you feel you understand the concept and are trying to implement it in your life, put a check mark in the space provided.

_____ Christian husbands and wives must communicate as equals in God's grace.

_____ Differences are the result of differentness, which is to be respected.

_____ In any difference of opinion, understanding is to be sought before an attempt is made at agreement.

_____ Understanding of the other person's point of view is most readily conveyed through "active-listening."

_____ Respect for the other person and his differences, and yourself and your differences, is most readily conveyed through "I" messages.

_____ Awareness of what's going on in yourself and your spouse is necessary for effective communication.

_____ Feelings are important clues to the issues that divide husbands and wives and should be used to guide them to the root issue (or issues).

_____ A healthy marriage is subject by both spouses to review in which each feels free to give a "state of the union" message whenever necessary.

_____ Change in a marriage of equals is best facilitated by a clear understanding of what specific change is needed and an agreement to change because you care.

_____ Change most readily takes place in an atmosphere of mutual respect and in a context of good-will.

_____ It takes two to communicate, therefore communication is impossible with crazymakers, manipulators, and others who try not to communicate.

# Notes

CHAPTER 1

¹Evelyn Millis Duvall, *Family Development* (Philadelphia: J. B. Lippincott Company, 1971), pp. 467–68.

²For more on the limits of the husband's authority, see my book *But I Didn't Want a Divorce* (Grand Rapids: Zondervan Publishing House, 1978), pp. 44–47.

³Paul Popnoe, *Family Life Magazine*, American Institute of Family Relations, Los Angeles (February, 1971), p. 2.

⁴Ibid.

⁵Eleanor Maccoby and Carol Jacklin, *The Psychology of Sex Differences* (Stanford: Stanford University Press, 1974), pp. 151–52.

⁶Patricia Gundry, *Heirs Together* (Grand Rapids: Zondervan Publishing House, 1980), p. 131.

CHAPTER 3

¹Jay Haley, *Strategies of Psychotherapy* (New York: Grune & Stratton, 1963), p. 11.

CHAPTER 4

[1]For more on the subject, see *Toward Effective Counseling and Psychotherapy: Training and Practice,* Truax & Carkhuff (New York: Aldine-Atherton, 1972).

CHAPTER 6

[1]Charles B. Truax and Robert R. Carkhuff, *Toward Effective Counseling and Psychotherapy: Training and Practice* (New York: Aldine-Atherton, 1972), p. 284.

[2]Brad Greene, Robert Isenberg, Duane Rawlins, Shayle Uroff, *Intra Family Communication Training: Parent's Manual* (Simi, Calif.: ICT Corporation, 1971), p. 3.1.

[3]Ibid., pp. 2.4 & 2.5.

[4]Truax and Carkhuff, *Toward Effective Counseling,* p. 286.

[5]Greene et al., *ICT Manual,* p. 3.17.

[6]Ibid., p. 3.1.

CHAPTER 7

[1]Statements adapted from the "Caring Relationship Inventory" by Everett L. Shostrom, published by the Educational and Industrial Testing Service, Box 7234, San Diego, CA 92107.

[2]Greene et al., *ICT Manual,* p. 4.13.

CHAPTER 8

[1]Ibid., p. 4.1. This is one of several techniques suggested.

[2]Ibid., p. 4.3.

[3]Sherod Miller, Elam W. Nunnally, and Daniel B. Wackman, with Ronald Brazman, *Minnesota Couples' Communication Program: Couples' Handbook* (Minneapolis: Minnesota Couples' Communication Program, 1972), pp. 41–42.

CHAPTER 9

[1]Ibid., p. 39.

CHAPTER 10

¹Greene et al., *ICT Manual,* p. 3.6.

CHAPTER 11

¹Ibid., pp. 111–14.

CHAPTER 12

¹*Aggression Lab,* pp. 118–19.

CHAPTER 13

¹Ibid., p. 25.
²See *You Can Change Your Personality,* p. 61, appendix A.
³*Aggression Lab,* p. 105.

CHAPTER 14

¹*Aggression Lab,* p. 207.
²Ibid.
³Ibid., pp. 207–19.
⁴Ibid., p. 221.

CHAPTER 15

¹Everett L. Shostrom, *Man, the Manipulator* (New York: Abingdon Press, 1967).
²André Bustanoby, *You Can Change Your Personality* (Grand Rapids: Zondervan Publishing House, 1976), p. 79.
³Ibid., p. 123.
⁴Ibid., p. 91.
⁵Ibid., p. 136.
⁶Ibid., p. 104.
⁷Ibid., p. 147.
⁸Ibid., p. 114.
⁹Ibid., p. 159.

[10]Paul Watzlawick, Janet Helmick Bevin, Don D. Jackson, *Pragmatics of Human Communication* (New York: W. W. Norton & Company, Inc., 1967), p. 51.

[11]Ibid., p. 54.

[12]Ibid., p. 57.

# Subject Index

# Scripture Index